Science: Sight, Light, & Color
Grades 5 to 8

LET'S INVESTIGATE

Book B: Sight, Light, & Color

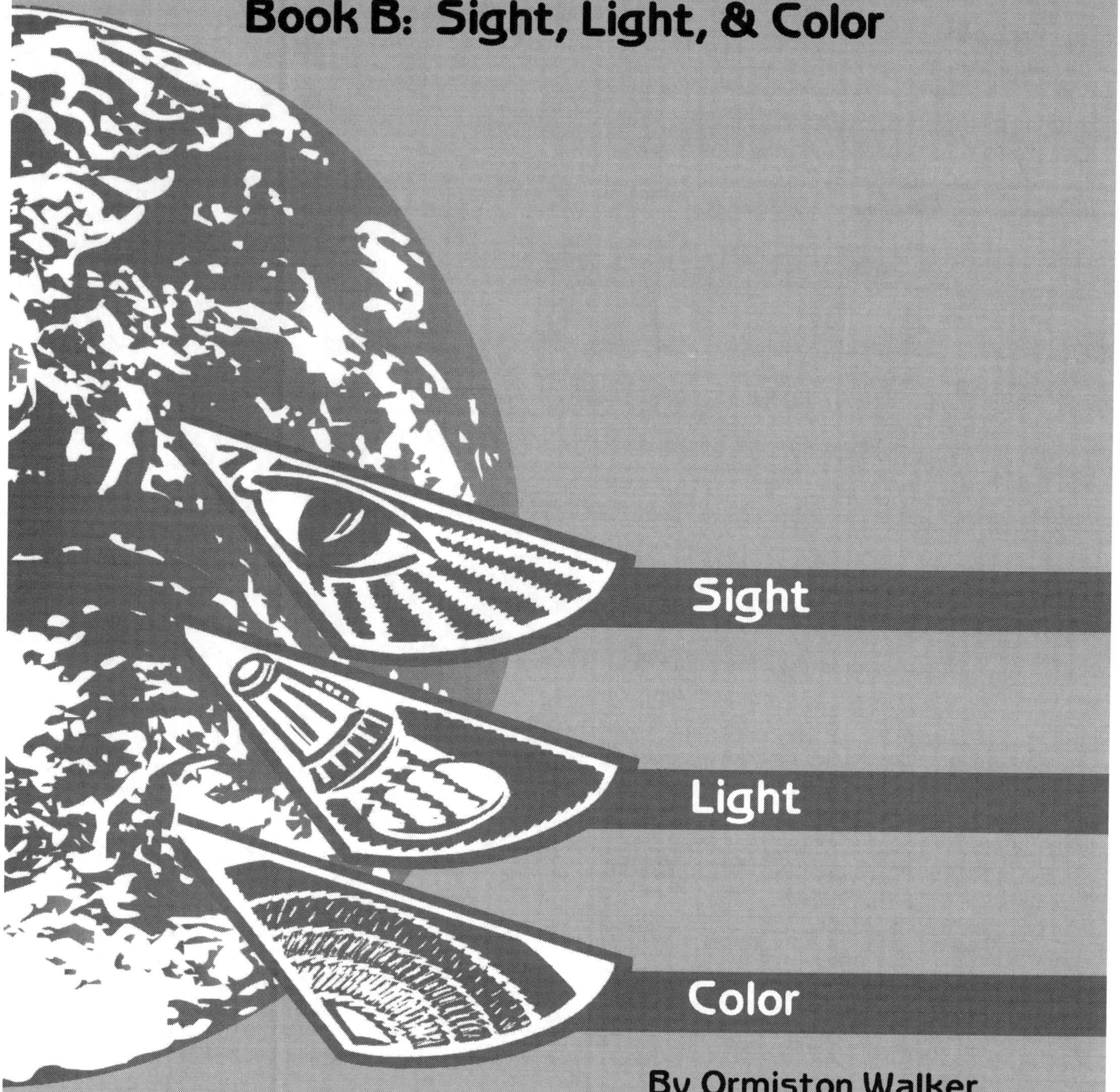

By Ormiston Walker

Published by Educational Impressions, Inc.

TITLE

Book Name: Let's Investigate
BOOK B: Sight, Light, & Color

AUTHOR

Ormiston Walker

ACKNOWLEDGEMENTS

Designer: Adrienne Morley, Digital Design
Illustrator: Geraldine Sloane
Editors: Pauline Scanlan and Jan Thornburn

ISBN Number: 978-1-56644-303-6

Revised Edition Published in 2008 by
Educational Impressions, Inc.
Hawthorne, NJ

website: www.edimpressions.com

Printed in the United States of America

Contents

SIGHT

How Do You Show an Optical Illusion?

WHAT YOU NEED:

- pictures (provided)
- art materials
- cardboard
- string
- adhesive
- nail
- plastic top of felt-tip pen
- small pane of glass
- jar of water
- candle

WHAT HAPPENS IN THIS ACTIVITY?

You're going to experiment with optical illusions and see how your eyes can play tricks.

Sometimes seeing can be deceiving. Can our minds always trust what our eyes seem to see? Sometimes we may not see things exactly as they are. Sometimes only part of what we look at is seen by our eyes: the rest is invented by our minds, based on what we already know. Minds can conjure up many illusions. These illusions came from our past experiences, associations, desires and imaginings. Some illusions are the outcome of errors in judgment. Can you remember any experiences like this?

WHAT TO DO:

Drawings that Mislead

- Look at Figure 1 (next page). Which line looks longer?
- Look at Figure 2. Which line looks longer?
- In Figure 3, which line, AB or CD, is longer?
- In Figure 4, which of XY or YZ is longer? How does line YW affect the eye?
- In Figure 5, which is greater, height or width?
- What about the birdbath in Figure 6?
- In Figure 7, which person is tallest?

  Now measure the lines of all the figures, checking whether you saw correctly. What do you find?
- Which of the two curved shapes in Figure 8 is larger? Measure them. What do you find?

Drawings that Shift

- In Figure 9, is the fold towards you or away? Turn the picture upside down. Do you still get the same effect?
- Look at the steps in Figure 10. How do they seem to shift?
- Turn them upside down. Describe what you see.
- What can you see in Figure 11?
- In Figure 12, how does the pattern jump between one design and another?

Figure 1.

Figure 2.

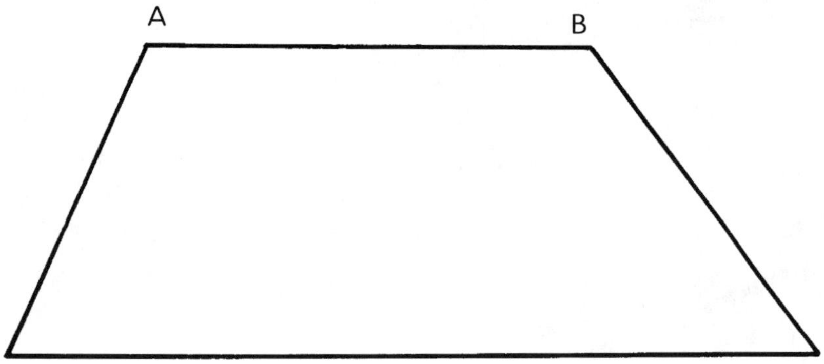

Figure 3.

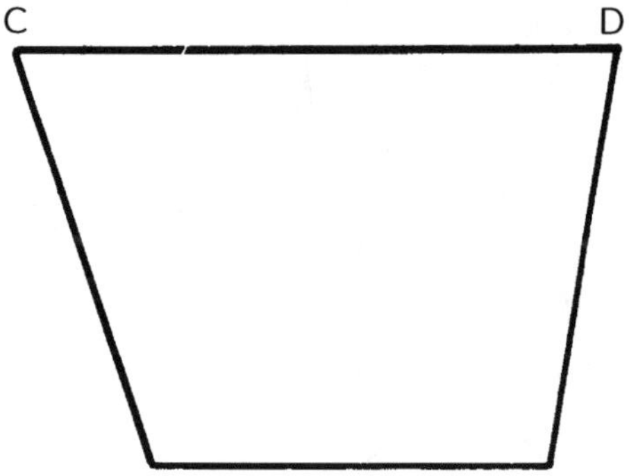

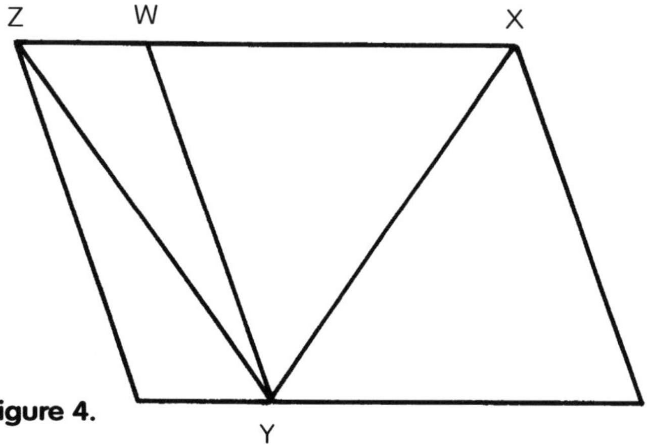

Figure 4.

Figure 5.

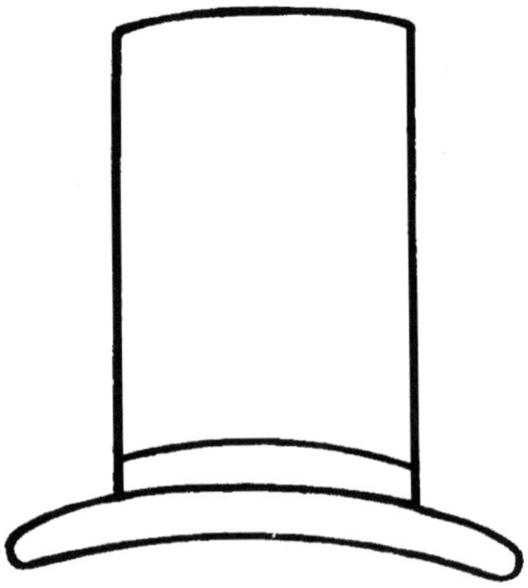

Figure 6.

Figure 7.

Figure 8.

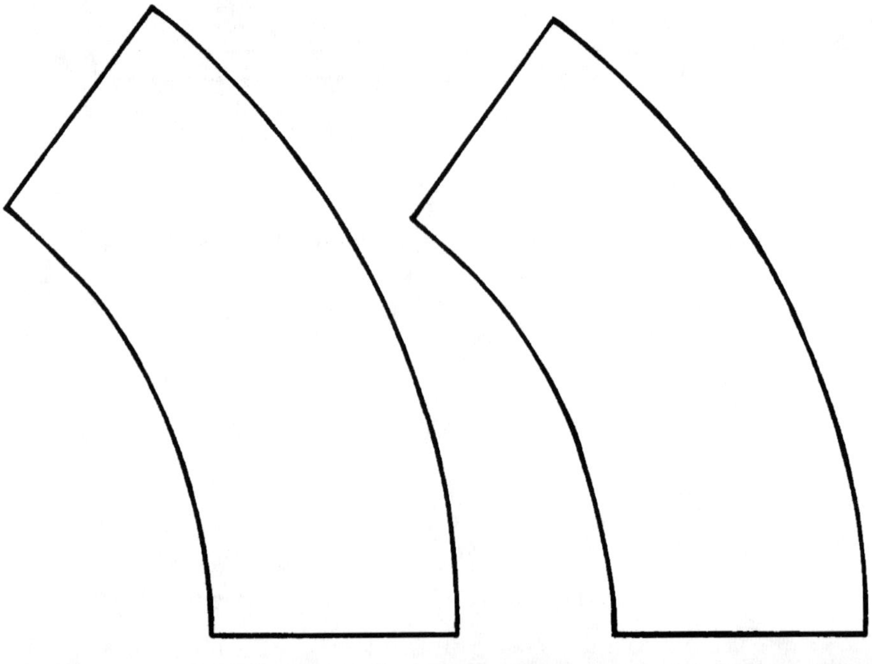

Figure 9.

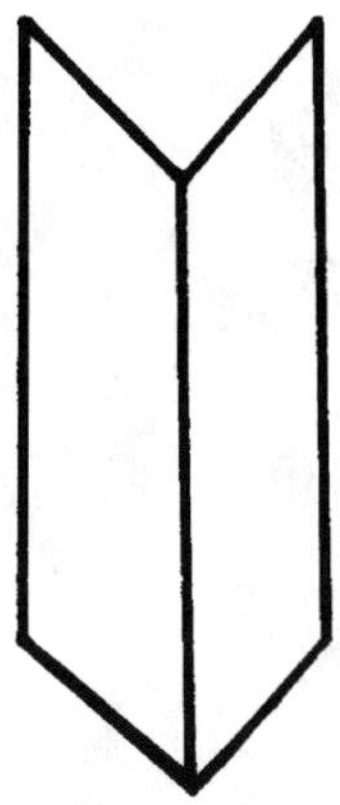

Figure 10.

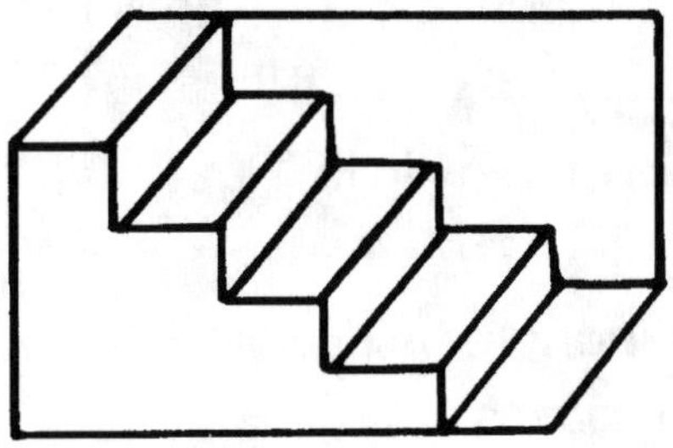

Figure 11.

Figure 12.

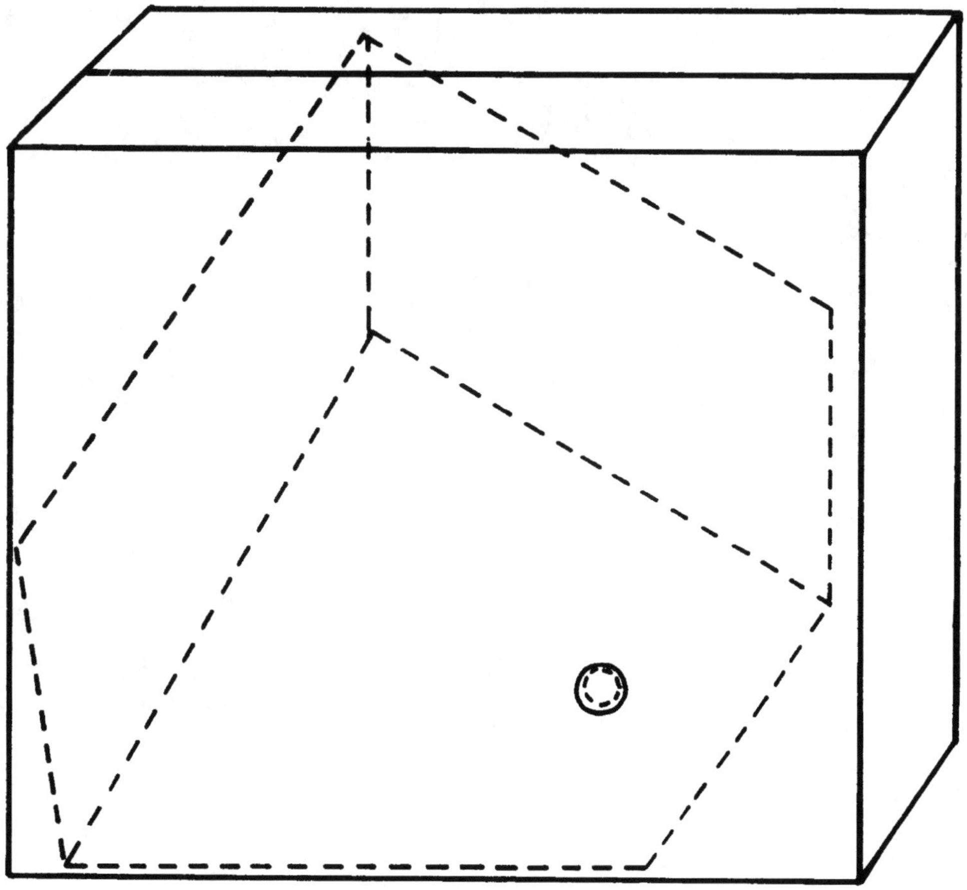

WHAT TO DO:

Some Other Illusions

- In pairs, set up the experiment shown in Figure 13 (next page). Together come up with a written comment on how the illusion of a candle burning in water works.
- Wave a flashlight or fireworks sparkler in a circle (Figure 14). Again in pairs, try to explain the "ring of fire" you see.
- Look at Figure 15. Make a Kanizas triangle by drawing an equilateral triangle and three black circles.

  Now cut from white paper another equilateral triangle exactly the same size. Paste this over the drawing so that each apex of the triangle is at the center of a black circle. Photocopy this and look at it carefully. What do you see? What happens when you reverse the black and white?

  This effect of seeing triangles which are not there is called **subjective contours**. Can you find some other examples of subjective contours in magazines?

Figure 13.

Figure 14.

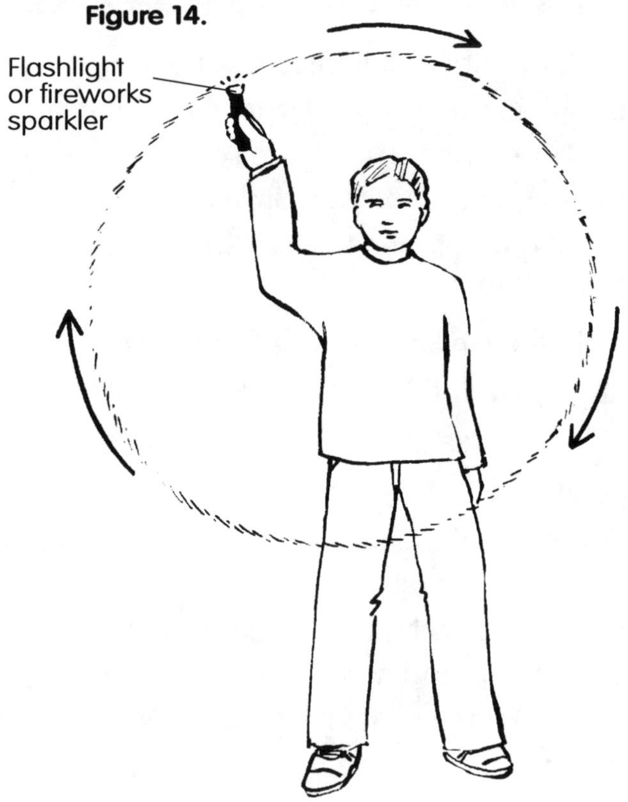

Figure 15.

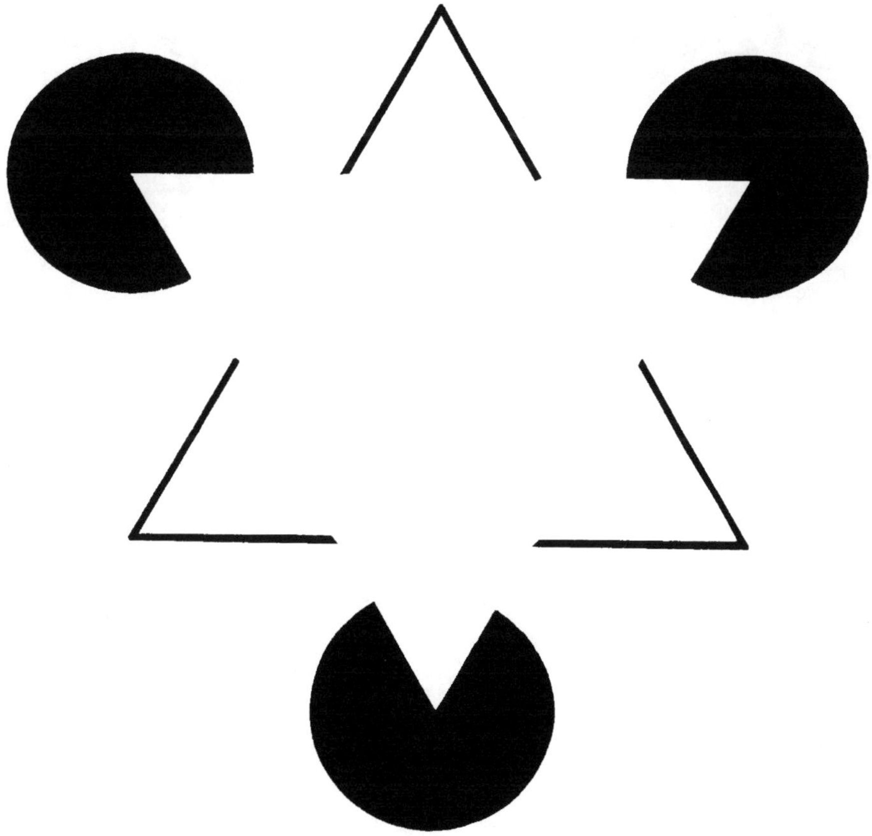

FURTHER INVESTIGATIONS:

- Look for other pictures showing that our eyes do, now and again, mislead us. For example, in Figure A (next page), look at the two circles. How do you explain that one looks larger than the other?
- Hold the circles in Figure B against strong light. What do you see?
- What impression do you get from Figure C?
- SCORE AT NETBALL! To show your skill at this, paste the drawings of Figure D onto light card, bend at the dotted line and paste the card so that the drawings are back to back. Make holes at the black dots, thread a string through and twirl the card. What's your score?

  This illusion happens because the image of the ball stays on the retina for up to 0.1 sec. after it has disappeared, in which time the net has come into view. This is called **persistence of vision** and is the basis of motion pictures.
- Find out about the work of artist Maurits Escher.
- Experiment with diagrams of your own that mislead our eyes.
- Do some research of your own into the structure of our eyes and the links with our brain. Try to come up with a concise explanation for the mystery of the optical illusion.

  Some key words to keep in mind are *optical Illusion, mirage, sight, visual,* and *eye.*

Figure A.

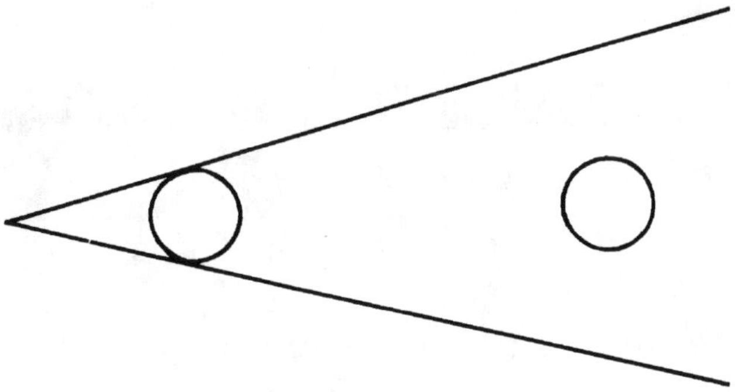

Figure B.

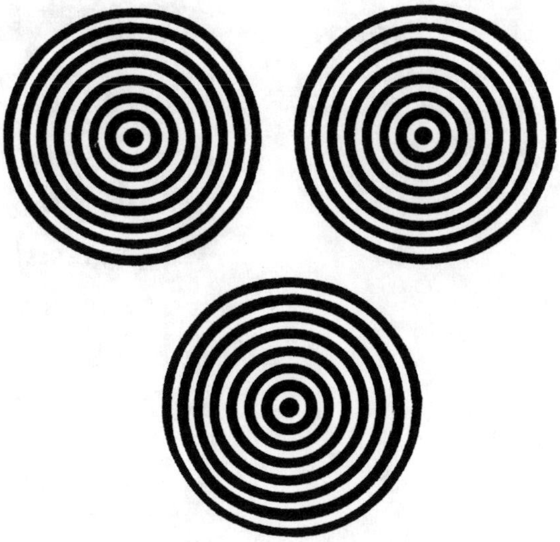

Figure C.

Figure D.

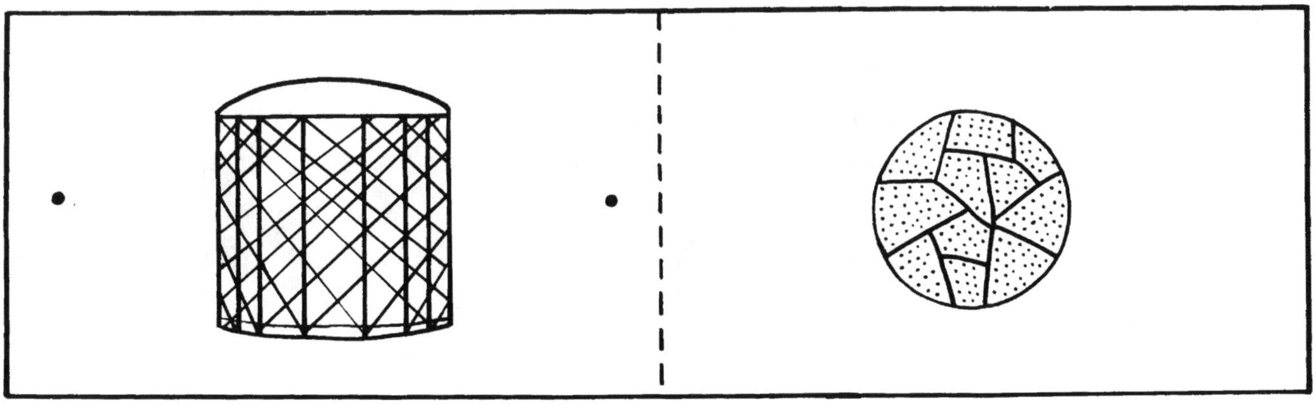

Let's Investigate

SIGHT

ACTIVITY 2:

Phantoms Before Your Eyes!

WHAT YOU NEED:

- two pencils

WHAT HAPPENS IN THIS ACTIVITY?

You'll see more objects than are actually there.

When you try this activity, you're going to see phantom fingers and phantom pencils. Why does this happen? Do the activity first and see if you can come up with an explanation of your own. Then have a look at the explanation offered at the end. No peeking first!

WHAT TO DO:

1. With the two pencils held level vertically and about 6 inches in front of the eyes, put the tip of one pencil against the top of the other.
2. Look at the far corner of the room through the pencils. You should see a phantom pencil. How does it come to be there?
3. Next, touch your first fingers together about 6 inches in front of your eyes. Now look past them at a far corner of the room. Where do those extra finger nails come from? Try to write 2-3 sentences of explanation before reading on.

Figure 1a.

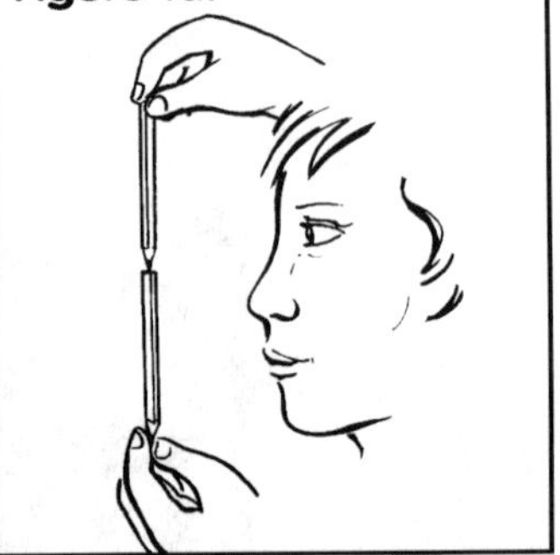

Figure 1b.

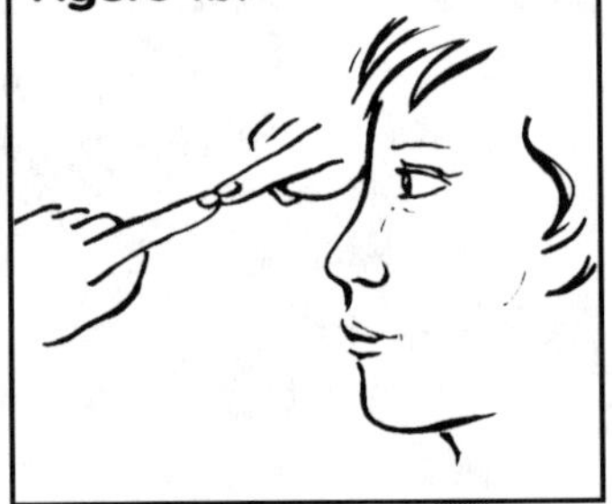

How does it happen?

An image of your fingers forms on the retina of your eye. At the same time an image of the far away corner forms. When your two eyes converge enough to fuse the two images of the corner, they are unable at the same time to converge to the angle needed to fuse together the two images of your fingers. The result is that the images of the two fingers overlap in such a way that they form a phantom finger with two fingernails.

WHAT TO DO:

Mirages

Look at this picture of a desert scene. The mirage of the desert is a phantom image. The palm trees appear to be reflected in water but there is in reality no water. The hot sand heats the air next to it, and a denser layer of air exists just above. The meeting place of the two layers of air acts like a lens, refracting or bending the rays of light from a far-away source giving the appearance of water. On a hot day, similar mirror-like reflections are seen over asphalt roads in summer. On coming closer the images are found to be nonexistent. Look out for these the next time you're in a car on a hot day.

Light from the top of the sand dune enters the cool air and bends away. On entering the hot air it bends further. The eye of the observer tracks the light beam back; therefore, the dune appears upside down coming from the ground and may look like a reflection in a pond or oasis.

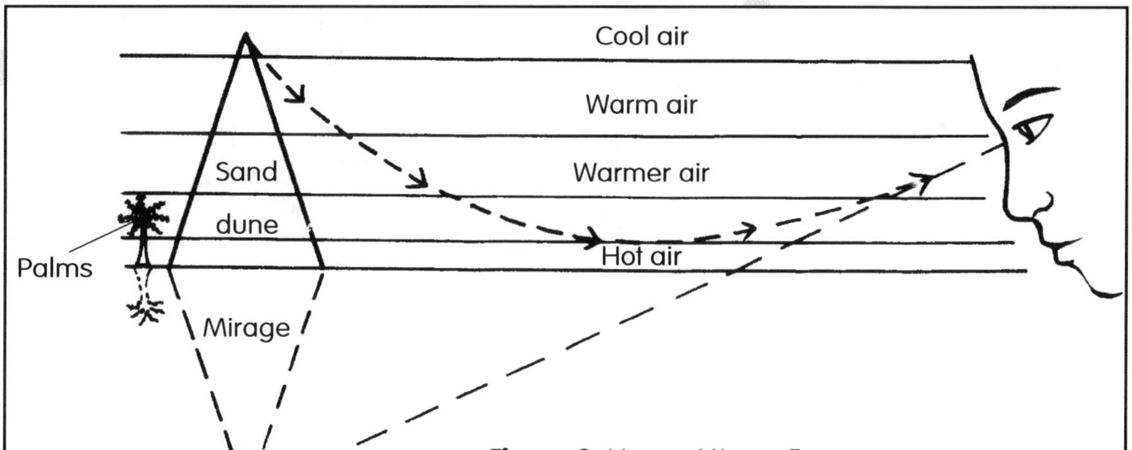

Figure 2. How a Mirage Forms

FURTHER INVESTIGATIONS:

- Try this. Punch three pinholes 1/16 inch (2 mm) apart to make a triangle on a piece of paper or card. Then, in another piece of paper or card, punch a single pinhole.

Figure 3.

Hold the card with the three holes close to an eye and the card with one hole about 2 inches (10 cm) in front of them. Now look through the three holes and the one hole at a strong light. How does the triangle look? Is it the same way up as on the card or is it upside down?

~ Is this an optical illusion, or is there an explanation?

- To see a mirage of your own making, stand with your hand on a brick wall which faces the sun on a hot, sunny day. Have a friend stand about 33 feet (10 meters) away holding a shiny metal pot or kettle in his hand. Watch for the appearance of a wall mirage.

~ Is the image clear or distorted? Can you explain this image.

Figure 4.

FURTHER INVESTIGATIONS:

- In the diagram of the human eye, Figure 5, some of the parts are named for you. On a sheet of paper, rule two columns: head the first column **Name of Part** and the second column **Function** (or What it Does). In the first column write the names of the parts given. In the second column, write what each part does. You will need to research the eye to do this properly.
- There are some parts of the eye not named in the diagram. Find out what these are and what their function is. Add this information to your two columns.
- When you observe the setting sun, you are also seeing something that is not there. Research the reason why.
- In certain parts of the world, in the late afternoon and early evening mountains can be seen looming out of the sea or above the horizon. Try and find out what causes these "looming" mirages.
- Write out definitions for these terms:

  ~ critical angle

  ~ total internal reflection.

  Explain in your own words how each plays a part in the formation of a mirage.

The Human Eye	
Name of Part	Function

Figure 5. The Human Eye

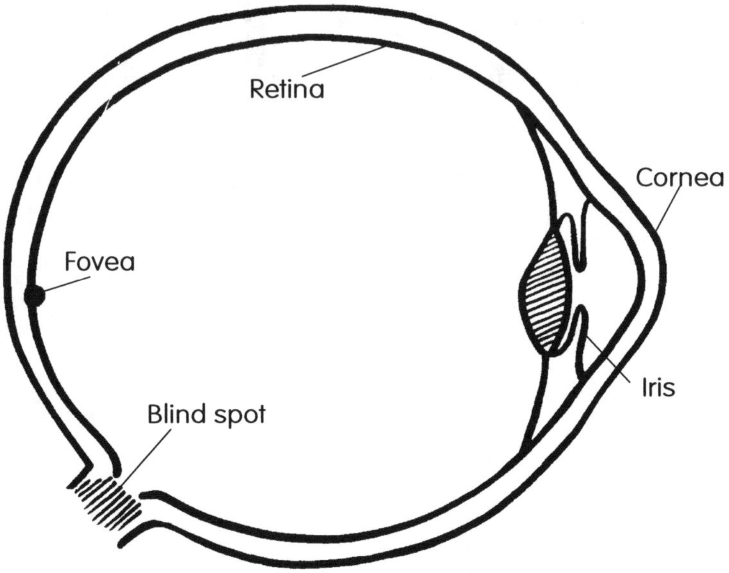

Let's Investigate
SIGHT
ACTIVITY 3:

Phantoms Before Your Eyes!

WHAT YOU NEED:

- card or paper tube
- tunnel diagram (supplied) Figure 2.
- card with small cross marked on it
- pin

WHAT HAPPENS IN THIS ACTIVITY?

In this activity, you seem to see through a hole in your hand.

Try closing one eye and looking at an object. Now try the same thing with the other eye. You saw the same object with each eye, right? So why, when you have both eyes open, don't you see the same object twice? Discuss what the possibilities might be in a small group before you read on!

The reason is, when you look at any object, your two eyes converge sufficiently to bring the two images on corresponding parts of the retina together. We call this focusing. You've probably been in a situation where an object seems out of focus because it's too close to your eyes. Nerves in the retina, stimulated by the image of the object, carry the pictures to the brain along the optic nerve. In the "seeing'"part of your brain, the two images are fused into one. Here's an activity which makes this point.

WHAT TO DO:

1. Take a cardboard tube or roll paper into a tube about an inch (3 cm) in diameter. Place the side of your hand next to the tube. Then with one eye look through the tube and with your other eye look at your hand. Do you seem to see through a hole in your hand?
   ~ Can you explain why in your own words?

Figure 1a. Look straight ahead, both eyes open.

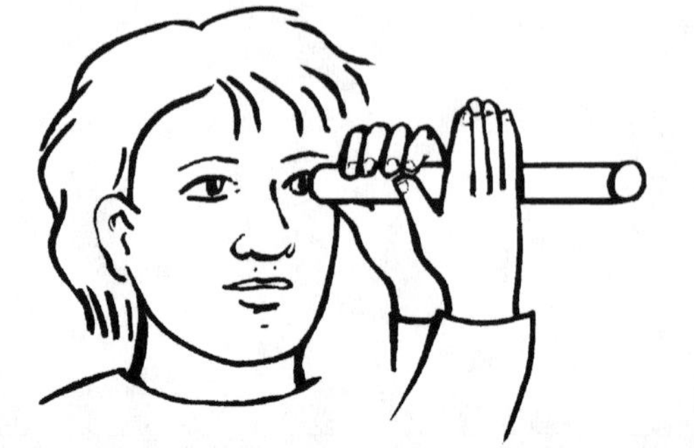

Figure 1b.

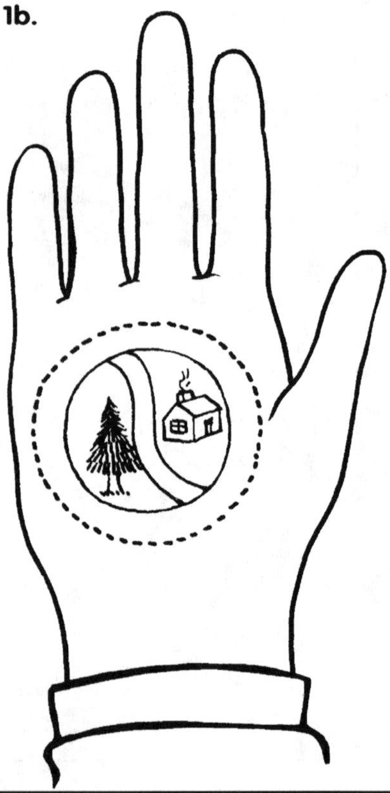

WHAT TO DO:

2. Hold the diagram of the tunnels (Figure 2) at arm's length from your eyes. Now slowly move it towards your eyes.

At a certain distance do you see a phantom tunnel? Why?

- ~ Now close your right eye? What happens?
- ~ Now close your left eye? What happens?
- ~ Can you explain this optical illusion?

Figure 2.

WHAT TO DO:

Figure 3.

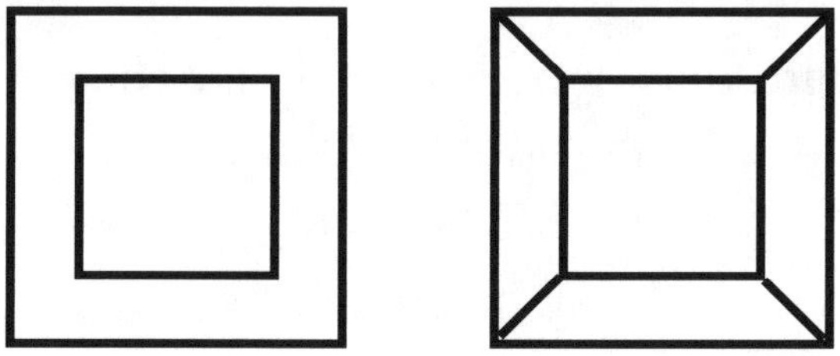

Figure 4a.

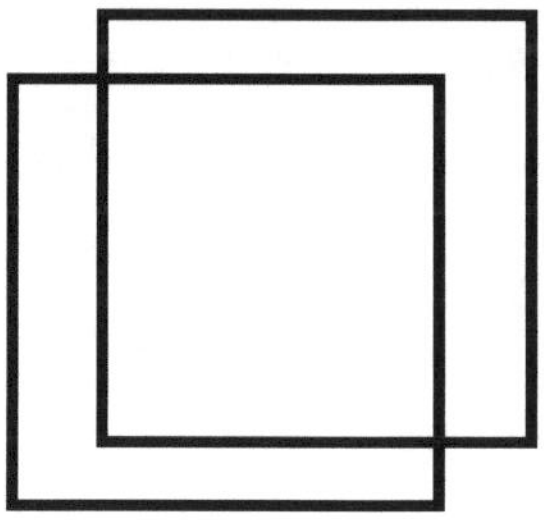

3. Pin a card with a cross marked on it to the wall, then stand an arm's length away. Move a forefinger to and fro in front of your eyes until you find a position where you cannot see the cross with both eyes open. Now bring your forefinger towards you with both eyes open. Do you appear to see the cross through your finger? How do you explain such an illusion?

4. Draw a .5 inch (1.5 cm) square inside a 1 inch (3 cm) square as in Figure 3. Then connect the corners and look at the figure steadily. Do the squares seem to shift, the inside square moving to and fro? There is no explanation for this. Can you think of one?

5. Draw two 1 inch (3 cm) squares as in Figure 4a. Then connect the corners and look steadily at your drawing. How does the appearance of the cube seem to change? Figure 4b.

Figure 4b.

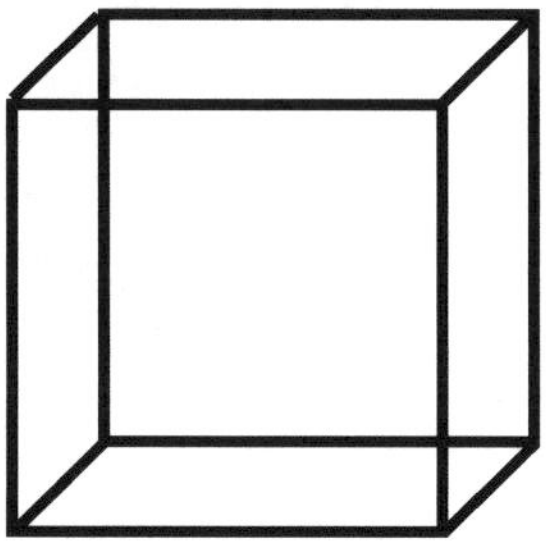

FURTHER INVESTIGATIONS:

- See if you can find a copy of a book **of optical illusions**. Have fun with them!
- Develop your own optical illusion. Try it out on your friends.

Let's Investigate
SIGHT
ACTIVITY 4:

Constructing an Illusion Room

WHAT YOU NEED:

- cardboard carton 40 x 40 x 38 cm with viewing hole and slot in roof as shown
- reading lamp
- strong white cardboard cut to sizes:
  Viewing Wall = 37 x 34 cm
  Wall 1 = 17 x 17 cm
  Wall 2 = 37 x 35 x 17 x 35 cm
  Wall 3 = 37 x 32 x 17 x 32 cm
  Floor = 38 x 34 x 35 x 18 cm
  (See templates supplied)
- adhesive
- templates for puppets, clowns, curtains
- 2 cm strips of plastic magnet
- flat iron, at least four pieces 3 cm square
- felt-tip markers
- paints or crayons
- scissors
- drill
- ruler
- plasticine
- two short pencils
- metal paper clips
- ping-pong ball

WHAT HAPPENS IN THIS ACTIVITY?

You'll see more objects than are actually there.

Have you ever been at a fun fair and stepped into a "crazy house" where rooms have been built with sloping floors and walls of different sizes? People usually find it difficult to keep their balance when walking through them because their expectations of what rooms should be like are tricked. These rooms work on the basis of optical illusion.

NOTE: *Templates are provided!*

WHAT TO DO:

1. To assemble your Illusion Room

a) Place the four cardboard walls against one another on a flat surface. Using the enlarged template, cut out the windows for walls 1, 2, 3 along the dotted lines.

b) Paste the windows to walls following carefully the instructions in Figure 1a. You have to place the windows in line with each other and with their upper edges parallel to the upper edge of each wall.

c) Use a photocopier to enlarge the floor template, Figure 1b. Then paste the enlargement to the cardboard floor.

d) Form the room by standing the walls upright and taping them together (see Figure 1a).

e) Set the room on the cardboard floor and fix it with adhesive. When the adhesive is dry, the room will be fixed in shape.

Figure 1a.

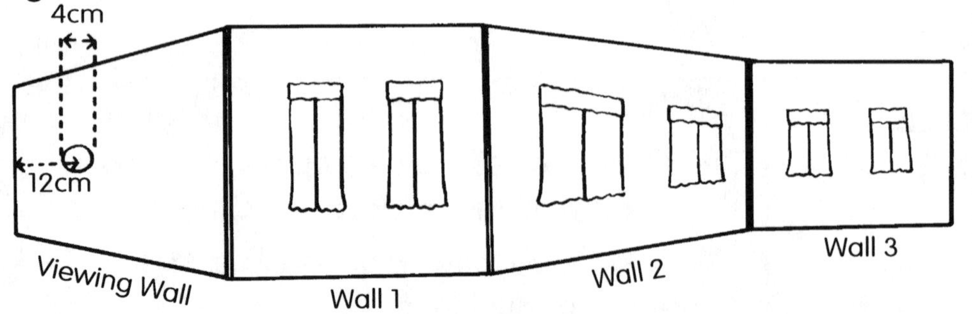

Walls of Illusion Room butted against one another and showing curtained windows in place. Paste windows to walls as shown. Smooth out any air bubbles.

Figure 1b.

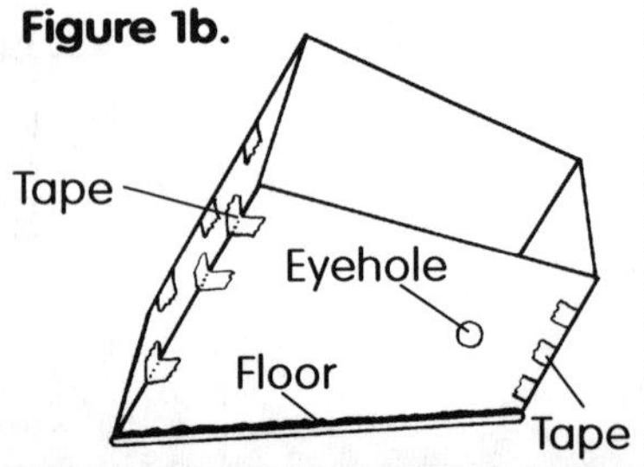

f) Cut or drill an eyehole 4 cm across as indicated in Figure 1a. Also cut or drill a matching eyehole in the carton.

g) Stick the puppets and clowns to light card and cut them out. Use adhesive to stick a plastic magnet to the back base of each puppet. Then place the magnet on a piece of flat iron so that the puppet stands upright. Balance clowns on pencils as shown. Place the room in the carton, close the top and place the reading lamp, switched on, over a slot.

h) You can also decorate the front of your room.

Figure 2

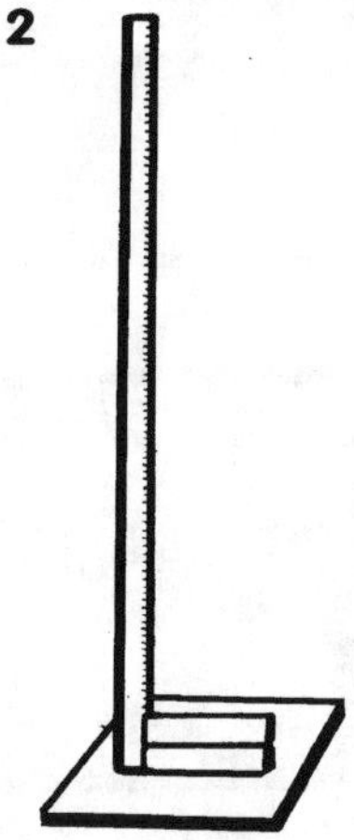

Figure 3

2. Look into your room through the eyehole.

~ What do you notice about the windows— the ones in front of you, those to the left, to the right?

3. Place the two puppets in the room making them wide apart and near the rear wall. What do you notice about them?

~ Repeat with the two clowns. Describe how they look.

4. Place the ping-pong ball in the left-hand corner and raise the room slightly to get the ball rolling along the back wall.

~ How far do you need to raise the room? Is it more or less than you might expect?

Figure 4.

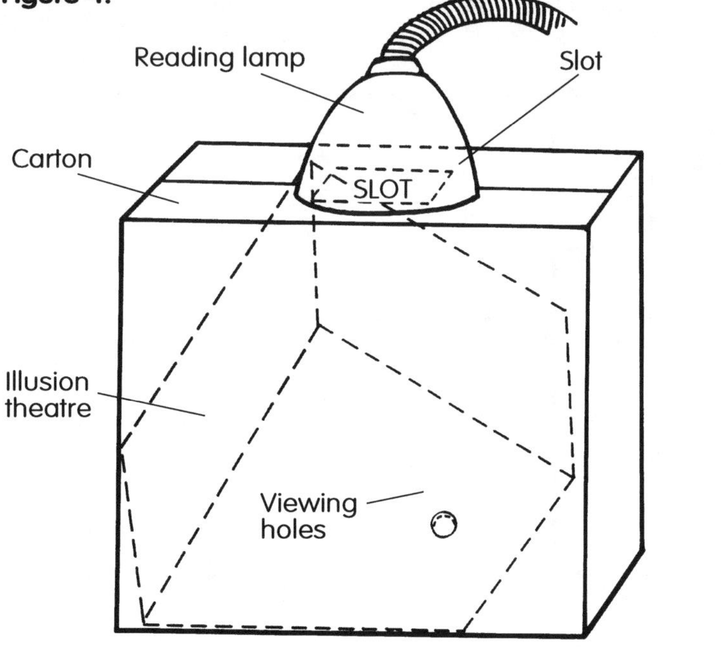

Windows for Wall 1
(Enlarge on photocopier 1.5 times)

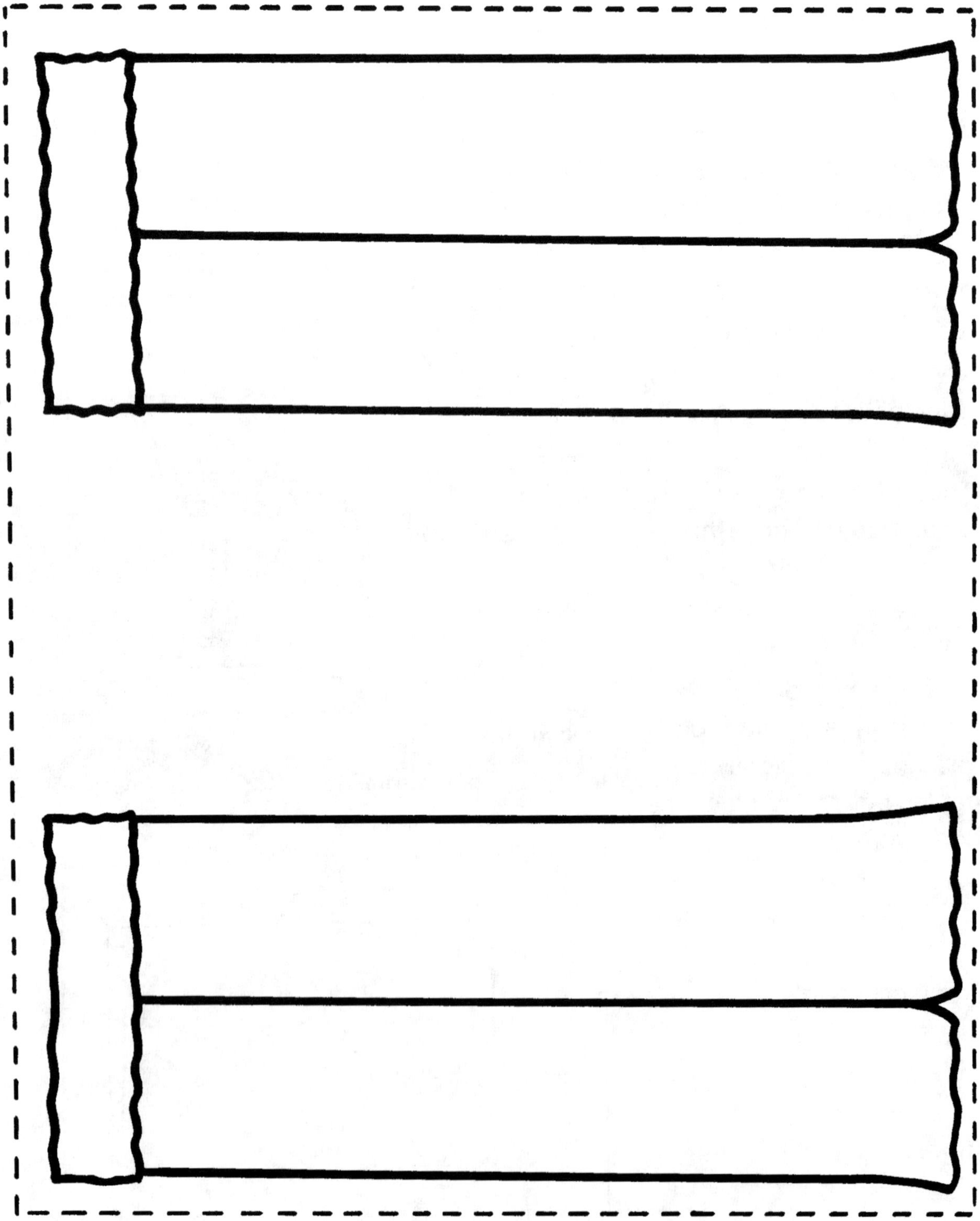

Windows for Wall 2
(Enlarge on photocopier 1.5 times)

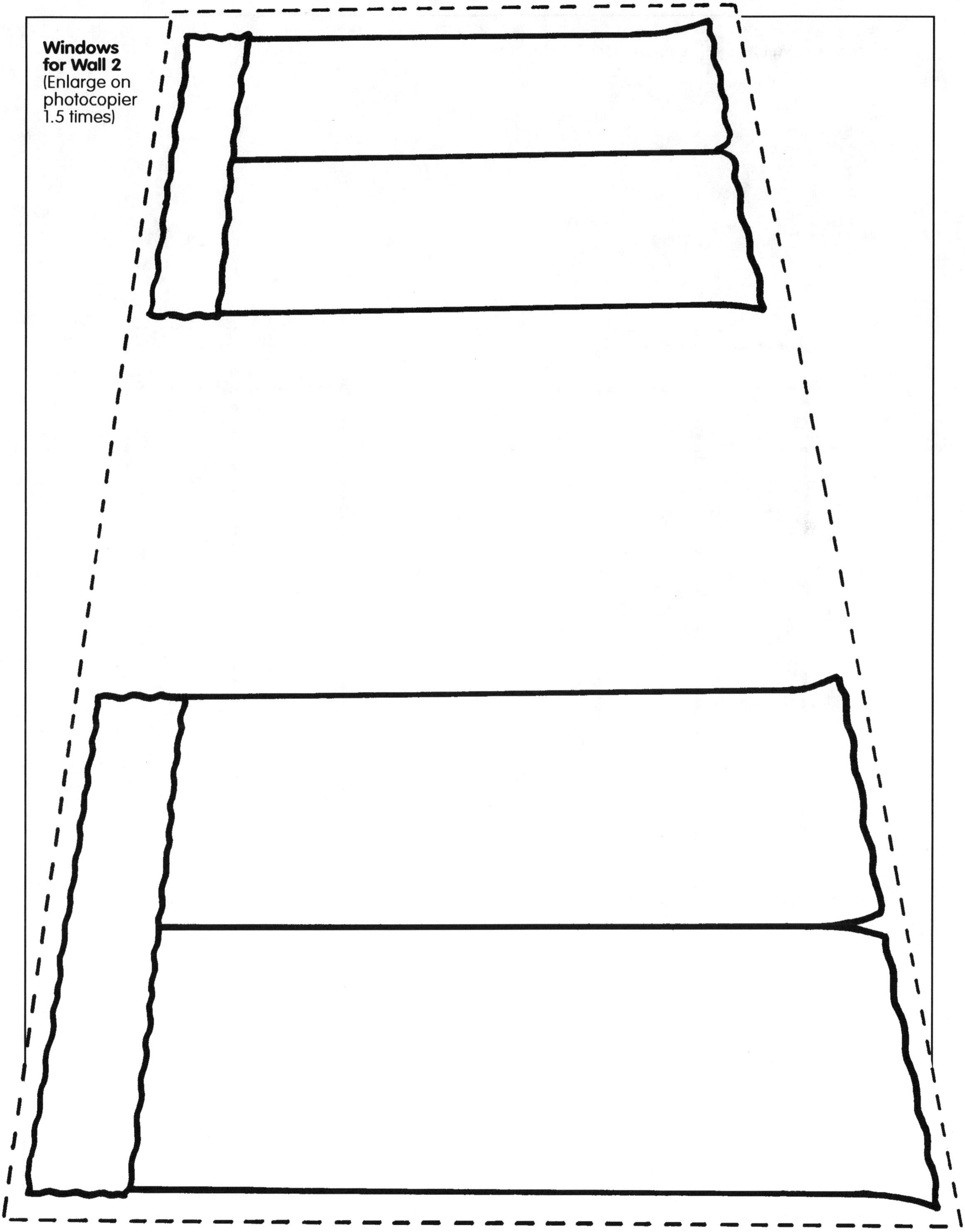

Windows for Wall 3 (Enlarge on photocopier 1.5 times)

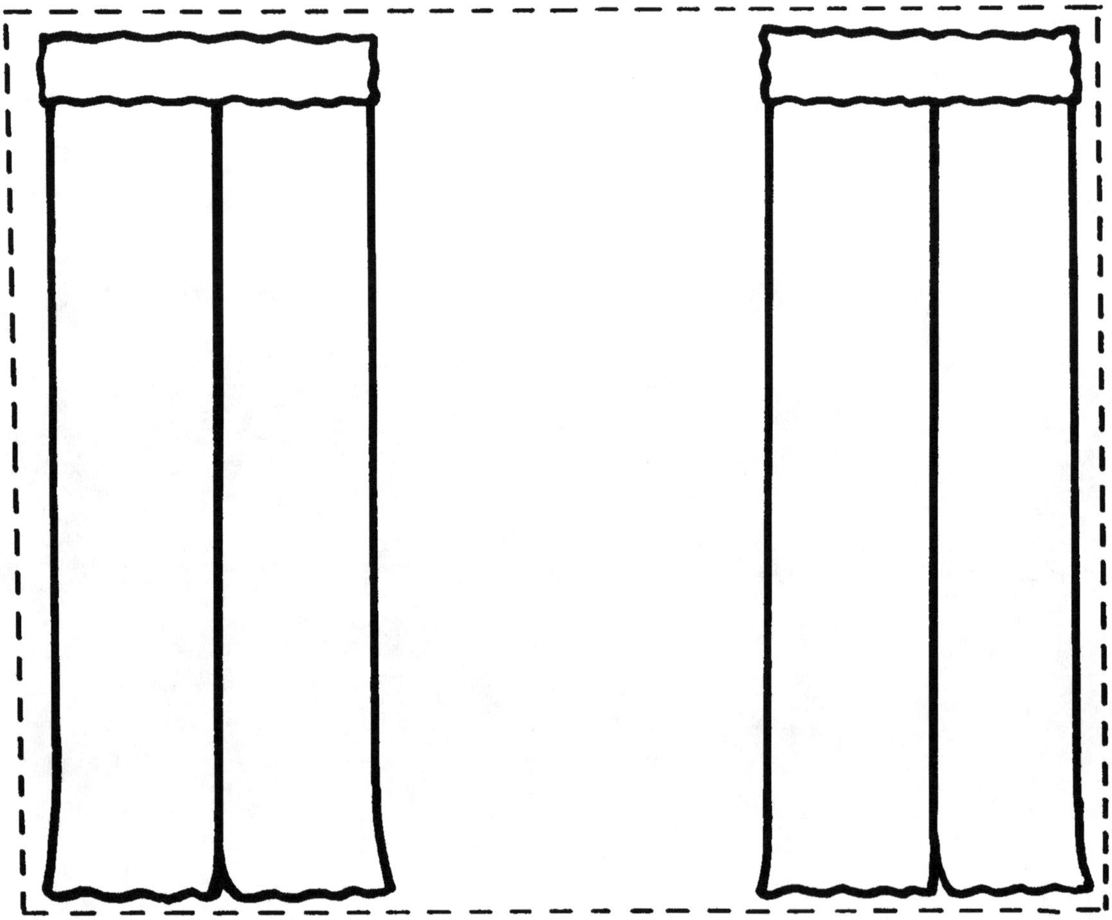

Floor (Enlarge on photocopier 2 times)

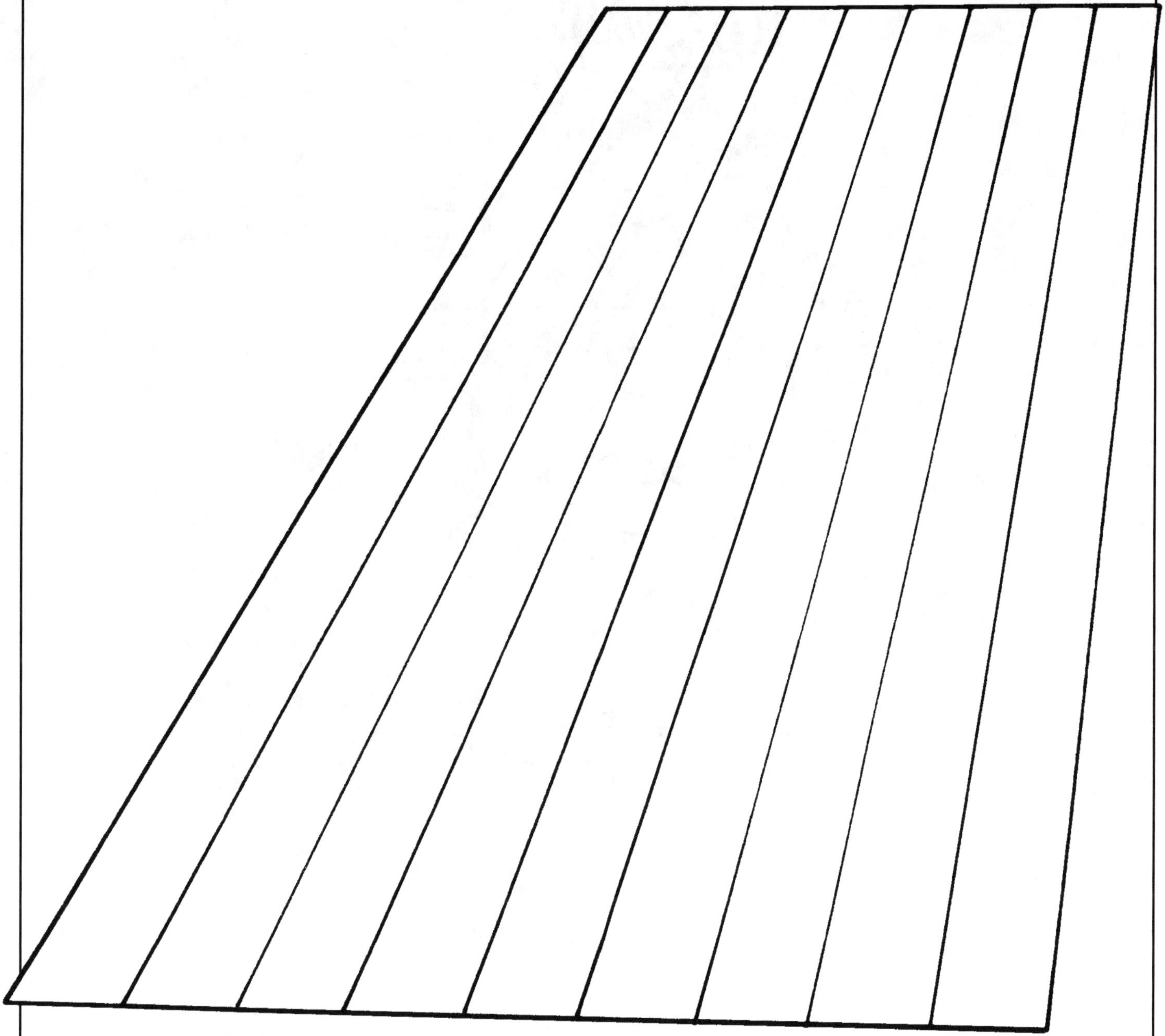

Puppet (Photocopy twice to make two puppets)

Clown (Photocopy twice to make two clowns)

FURTHER INVESTIGATIONS:

- Design some other shapes and activities for your Illusion Room. Try magicians, trees, tinsel figures, T.V. stars or sports heroes. Replace the rear curtains with clear cellophane. How different do the shapes look when viewed through this?
- Put your Illusion Room on display at a science fair so that visitors can see it and experiment with it. By having the room inside the carton, the odd shape of the room is not given away and you will get the best responses from your viewers.
- At amusement parks, fun fairs, (and also at University Departments of Engineering - Seismology Studies), an Illusion Room or Platform is rocked by a mechanism just as a boat is rocked at sea or an aircraft tosses in a storm. This can produce motion sickness, nausea and dizziness in the person.

  While looking inside your room, have a friend rock it gently to and fro, then more vigorously. Do you find yourself starting to rock to and fro also? How do you feel? Research which body mechanisms are affected, producing the sensations of motion sickness.

LIGHT

Let's Investigate
LIGHT
ACTIVITY 5:

Can You See Light?

WHAT YOU NEED:

- wooden box 30 x 30 x 60 cm (12 x 12 x 24 ″)
- black cloth
- flat black paint
- picture glass*
- black paper
- flashlight or projector
- scissors
- lenses
- color filters
- cardboard
- dish
- incense cone (for smoke supply)
- flat-shape bottle
- water
- plasticine
- mirror
- brush
- Cellotape
- workshop tools

* Take care when handling glass. Wear gloves.

THIS REQUIRES ADULT SUPERVISION.

WHAT HAPPENS IN THIS ACTIVITY?
You make a smoke box to study light.

It might seem a bit obvious, but you wouldn't be able to see much if we didn't have light. But what is light? The next time you switch on a lamp, think to yourself, "What am I seeing?" What you see, of course, are the objects that become visible when light strikes them. But can you actually see the light or just the objects? It is possible to see light. The sort of light that is easiest to see is the light that forms into rays.

You can observe light rays by darkening a small room when the sun is shining against a window. Tape sheets of black paper to the window and in the center sheet, cut three holes about 3 cm across. When the only light coming into the room is through the three holes, shake some baby powder or chalk grains to create a dust in the path of the light. The light entering the room will illuminate the tiny particles of dust and you will see the beams of light standing out clearly. A better way to study light is to make a smoke box in which you can keep the smoke under control continuously.

WHAT TO DO:

1. Replace the back of your box with two curtains of black cloth, overlapping in the middle and hanging loosely. This enables you to put your hand in the box and move things around without too much smoke escaping. Paint the inside of the box with flat black paint and fit panes of picture glass into the top and front sides of the box. **Ask an adult to help you with this.** At the righthand end of the box, cut a central opening 8 cm tall by 5 cm wide. In the mid-line of a piece of black paper, cut three holes in a row, each about 0.5 cm square. Tape this over the opening as in the diagram, Figure 1.

Figure 1.

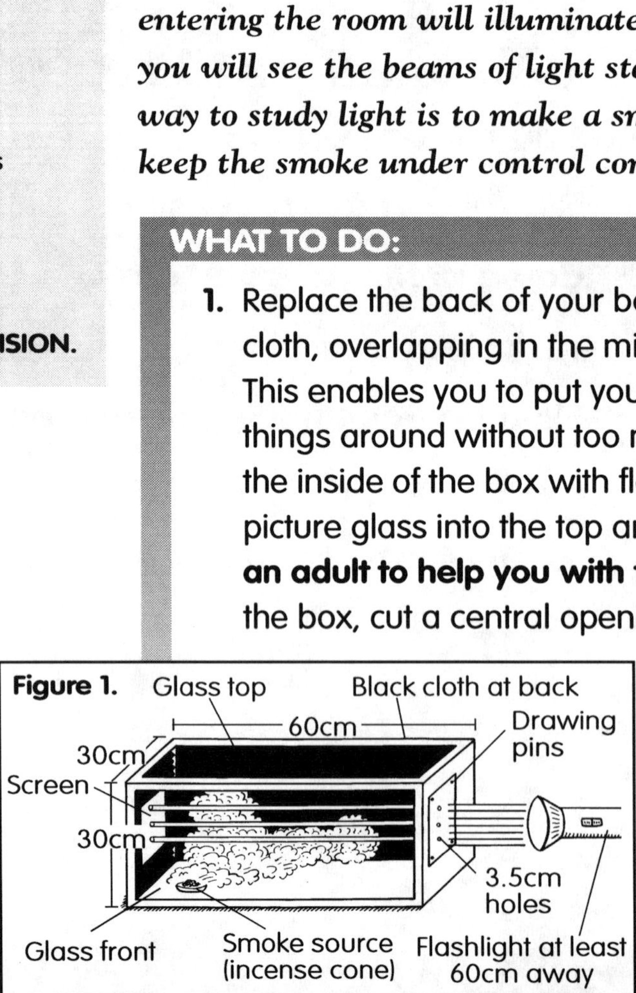

WHAT TO DO:

2. To use your smoke box, let an incense cone smoulder so that the box contains smoke. Then arrange a flashlight or projector to give a parallel beam set in position as shown in the diagram. A strong light beam is necessary for good results. Observe the light rays. What does this demonstrate to you about light rays?
3. Use the smoke box for the following demonstration experiments:
   a) Reflection of light. Figure 2.
   b) Refraction of light. Figure 3.
   c) Action of a lens on light rays. Figure 4.
   d) How a lens forms an image. Figure 5.
   e) A concave lens diverges or spreads out the light rays. Figure 6.
   f) Experiments with color. Figure 7.

Figure 2.

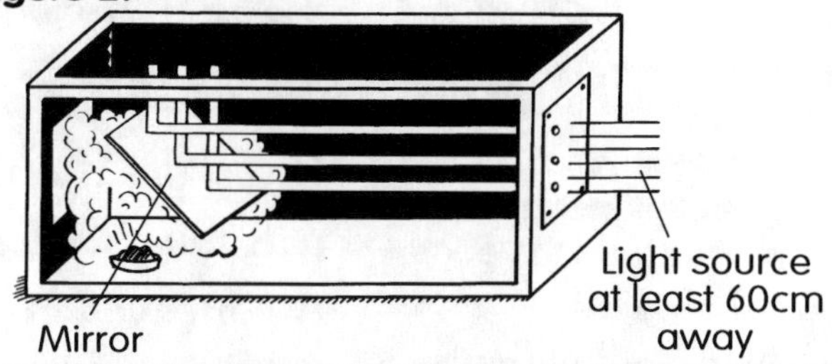

Figure 3. Tape a new piece of black paper over the opening as shown. Make only one hole in the paper this time.

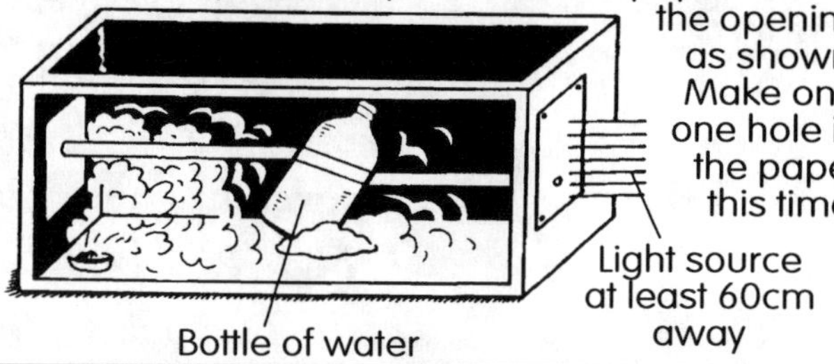

Figure 5.

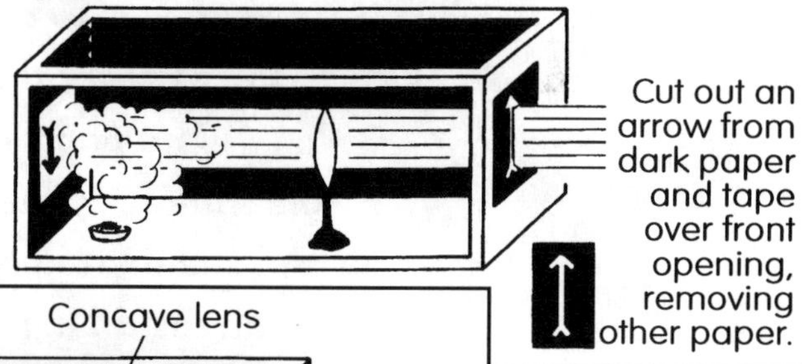

Figure 4.

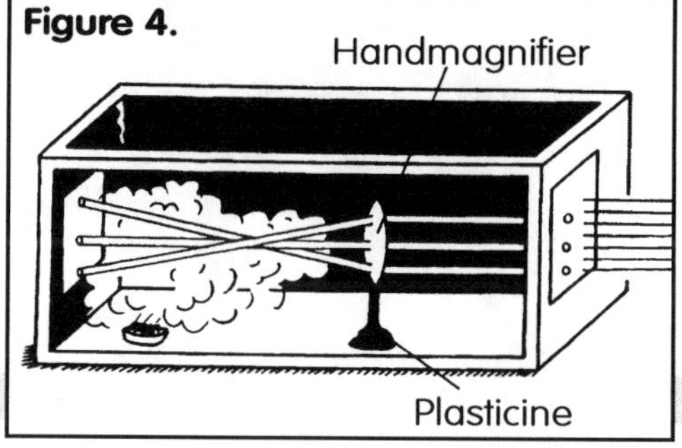

Figure 6.

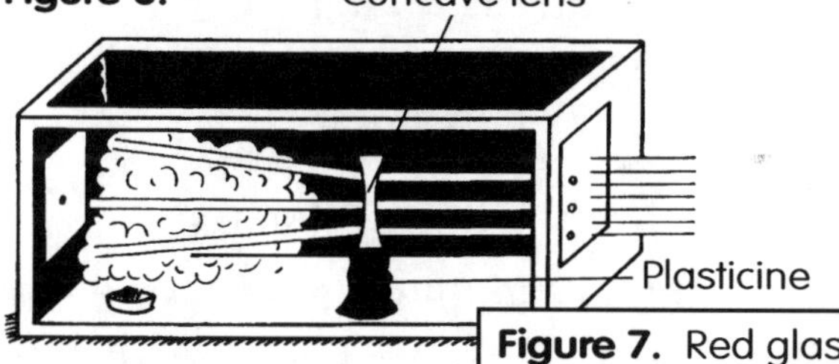

Figure 7.

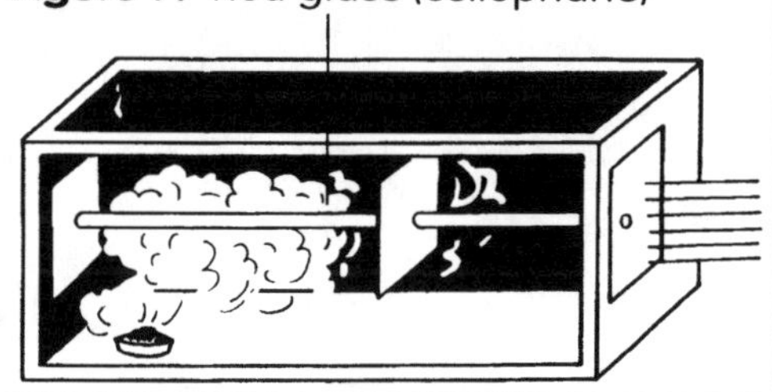

FURTHER INVESTIGATIONS:

- Do light rays always travel in straight lines? Einstein said that when light rays from a distant star graze the edge of the sun, the strong gravity field of the sun bends or deflects the light rays in their paths. Scientists call this effect "gravitational lensing." Research this further and write a paragraph about it.

Figure 8.

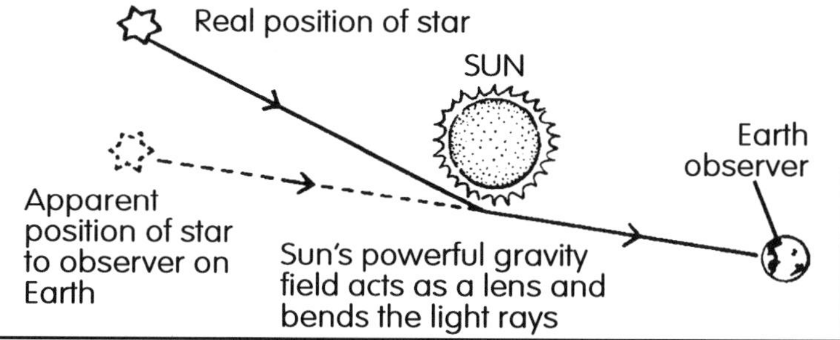

Let's Investigate
LIGHT
ACTIVITY 6:

What's a Concave Lens?

WHAT YOU NEED:

- glass with a concave base (thinner at the middle than the edge)
- white paper
- short piece of candle
- wire
- water
- page of print
- dark room

WHAT HAPPENS IN THIS ACTIVITY?

You experiment with a concave lens.

If you did the smoke-box experiment,you will have worked with a concave lens A concave lens is a hollowed-out lens, thinner at the middle than the edges. You see concave lenses everywhere, especially in the eyeglasses of shortsighted (myopic) people.

They work by parallel light waves striking the lens and spreading out, as shown in Figure 1. It will help if you look at Figures 1 and 2 as you read this explanation.

The point F from which the spreading rays appear to come is the focus of the lens. The point O is the middle of the lens and the distance OF is the focal length. If AB is an object, then the parallel light rays from A and B diverge (spread apart) on leaving the lens to points D and G. The spreading rays from A and B will seem to come from a and b and the eye sees a smaller upright image ab of the object AB.

Figure 1.

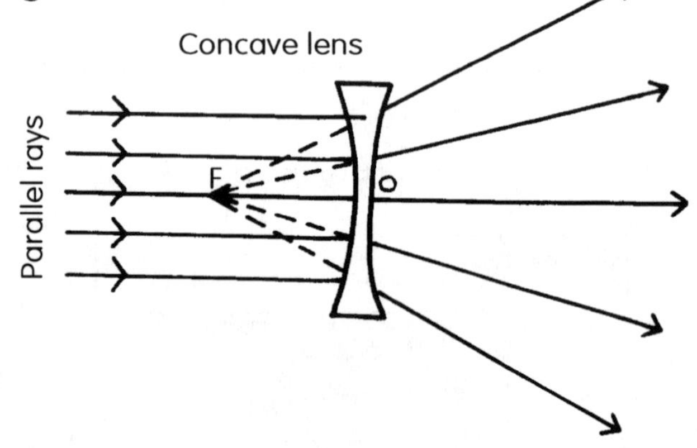

Figure 2.

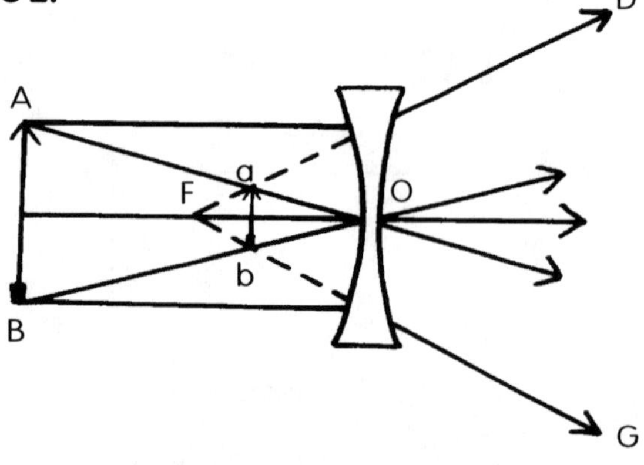

In shortsighted people, the concave lens of their eyeglasses acts as the support for the retina, which is usually further away from the lens in their eyes than for most people. This means that the image that falls on the retina of shortsighted people is out of focus. The concave lens of eyeglasses helps to refocus the image at a shorter distance.

WHAT TO DO:

Figure 3a.

1. Look through the base of the glass at your fingers and other objects. What do you notice about them. Describe the images.

Figure 3b.

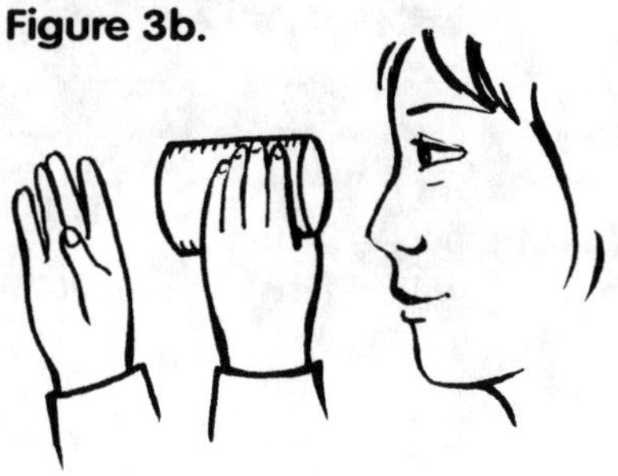

2. In a darkened room, place the glass on its side and light the short piece of candle near its mouth.
   ~ What does the concave base of the glass do to the light? Can you now explain why a concave lens is described as a "diverging lens"?

Figure 4.

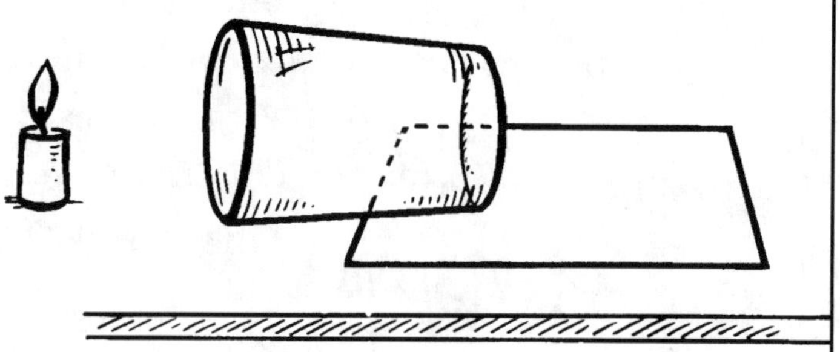

FURTHER INVESTIGATIONS:

- See if you can get hold of a pair of opera glasses. What lenses are used in these? What is their purpose?
- Make a tiny loop in the piece of wire and lift out a drop of water. Look at this print through the drop. How is the water drop acting as a lens? What kind of lens? Now try removing some of the water by touching a finger to the water surface.
  ~ Now look through the drop again at the print. How is it different? What kind of a lens is the water drop acting as now?
  ~ Draw the light rays for the two types of lenses.

Figure 5.

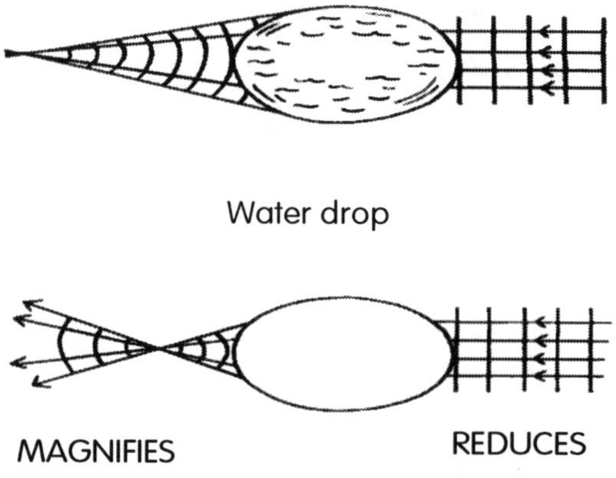

Can a Bottle Act as a Lens?

WHAT YOU NEED:

- transparent tall glass bottle 1-1.5 liter capacity with a flat base
- candle
- water
- white card

WHAT HAPPENS IN THIS ACTIVITY?

You prove how a bottle can be used as a lens.

In glass, the velocity (speed) of light is about ⅔ its velocity in air, while in water its velocity is about ¾ its velocity in air. Because glass is more dense than water, it slows up light by a greater amount.

In the following experiment you will see how the water in the tall bottle acts as a cylindrical lens. The thick glass in the base of the bottle slows the light most at the middle where it is thickest. At the sides, the glass is thinner and the light is least slowed. This changes the straight, parallel wave fronts into curved, concave wave fronts, which converge to a focus near the bottle.

The water has the same cylindrical shape as the bottle it is in and so exerts an effect similar to the glass. Again, the straight parallel wave fronts are changed into concave wave fronts. But these are not so sharply curved as with glass because water slows light less than glass does. The concave wave fronts converge to a focus further away from the bottle than they do with glass.

Figure 1.

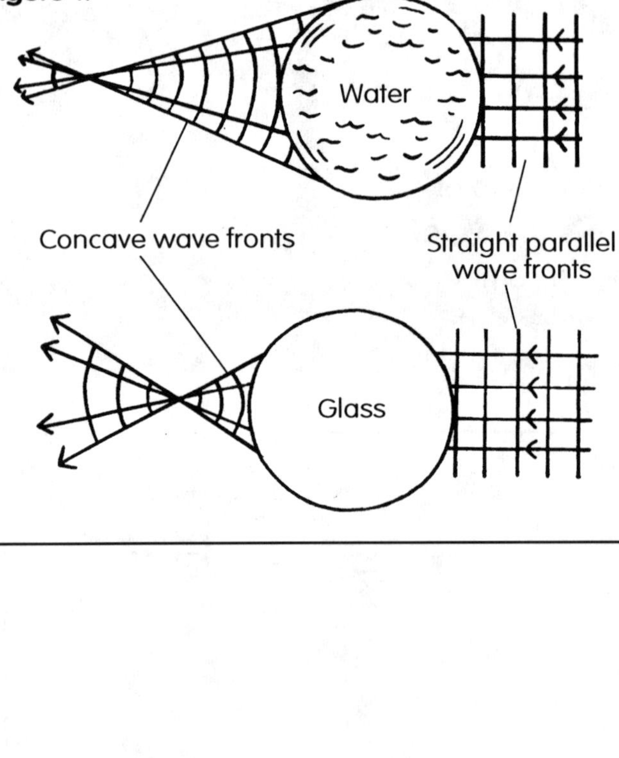

WHAT TO DO:

1. Hold a bottle of water near your eyes and place your other hand at various distances behind it.
   ~ When your hand is close to the bottle, how do your fingers look? How do they look at about 5 cm (2 inches) away? Move your hand still further away. Describe how your hand looks now.

Figure 2.

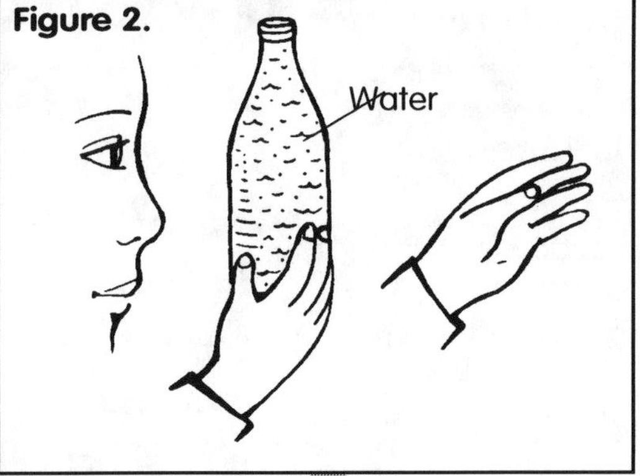

2. Place the bottle on a piece of white card. Next put a lighted candle about 20 cm (8 inches) away from one side of the bottle.
   ~ What do you see the light rays doing on the other side of the bottle? What is the name for the point where the light rays cross?

Figure 3.

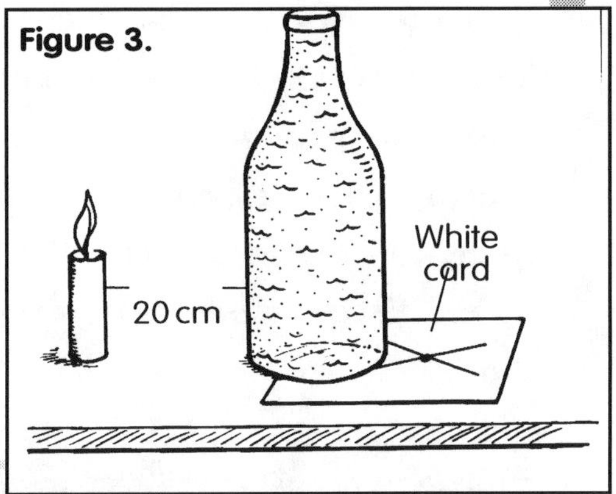

FURTHER INVESTIGATIONS:

- Do a survey on how many people in your grade at school are shortsighted. Find out how they correct their vision.
- As people get older they often become farsighted. What does this mean? How do they correct their vision?
- Find out what optometrists do.

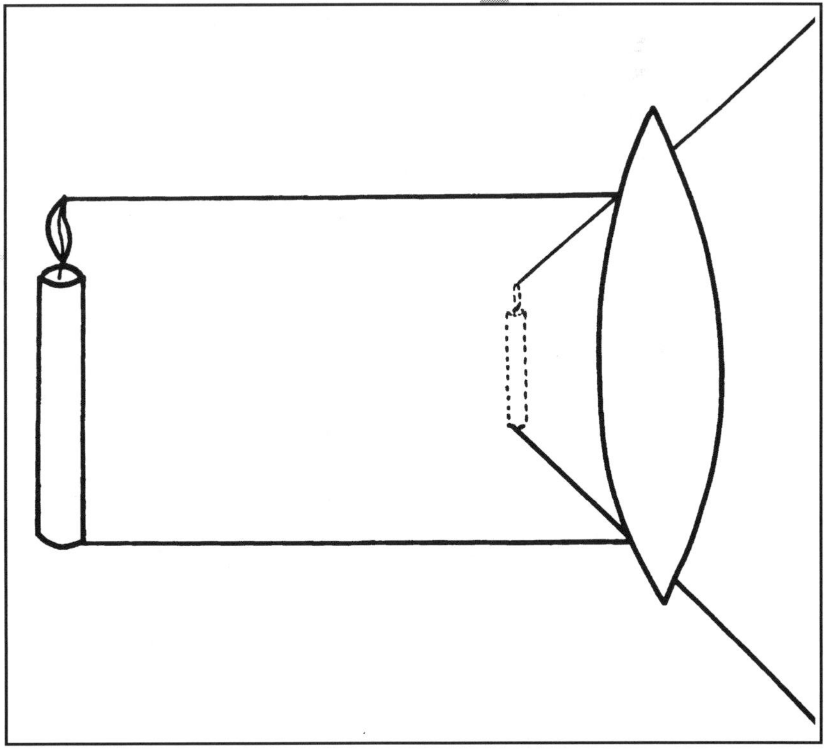

Tricks With a Fishbowl!

WHAT YOU NEED:

- round fishbowl
- water
- white paper or card for screen
- chalk dust or talcum powder
- matches

Note: Depending upon the age of the students, this may require adult supervision.

Lenses bend light rays out of their straight path. This is what our eyes do. They are natural lenses. By bending light rays, our eyes bring the rays to a sharp focus and enable us to see clearly (unless we're shortsighted!). Birds' eyes do this particularly well; we say they have keen sight. Insect eyes do it poorly and they see only blurred shapes. Cameras, binoculars and refracting telescopes bend light to a focus by using a lens. They bring light rays from distant objects to a focus so making it possible for us to see the object clearly.

WHAT HAPPENS IN THIS ACTIVITY?

You make and experiment with a spherical lens.

WHAT TO DO:

Figure 1.

Figure 2.

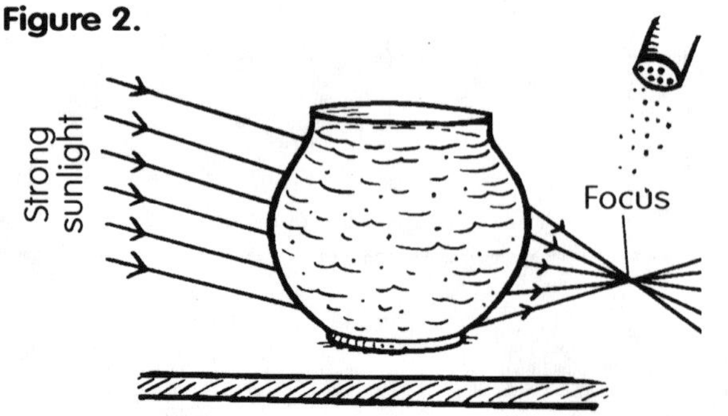

1. Fill the round fishbowl with clear water. Have a friend sit with his or her face in bright sunlight and hold the bowl about a meter (3 feet) away in the shade. Move the paper screen to and fro on the other side of the bowl. Describe what you see.
2. Arrange the bowl so that strong sunlight falls on it. Then sprinkle or shake fine chalk dust or talcum powder behind the bowl. What do you observe? What happens to the light rays?

WHAT TO DO:

3. Hold a piece of dark paper at the focus.
   - ~ What happens? Can you explain why?
   - ~ Why did we use dark paper?
   - ~ Try holding your palm at the focus. What do you feel?
4. Carefully hold a match-head at the focus.
   - ~ What happens?

Figure 3.

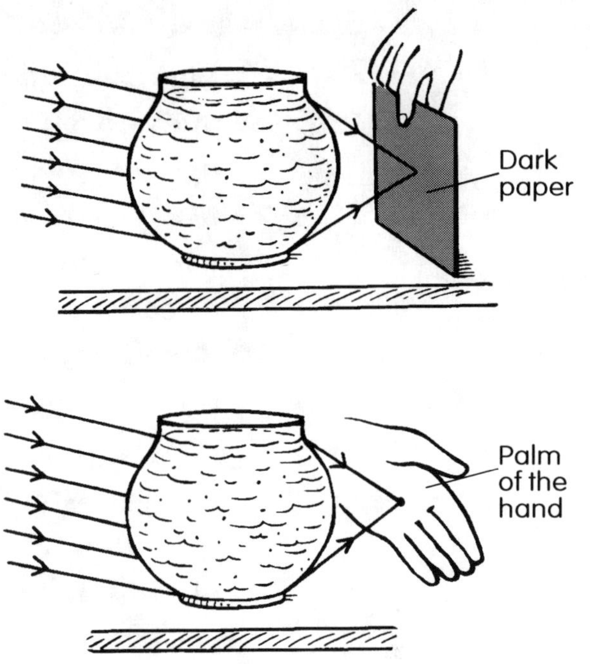

Figure 4.

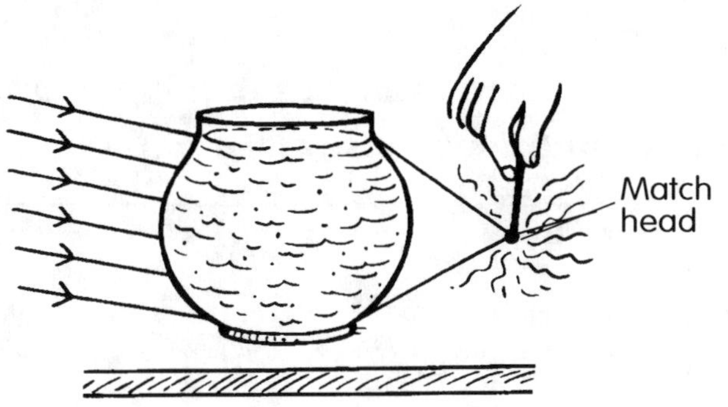

FURTHER INVESTIGATIONS:

- Besides adjusting for distance, eyes also need to adjust for dim or bright light. Cats' eyes open wide at night to let more light in.

  Roll several sheets of paper into a hollow cylinder and place this on the print of a book so that you are trying to read in the darkness. How long before you can see the print? Now look quickly into a mirror, closely watching your pupils as you do this.
  - ~ What happens to the pupils? Why?
- Research how owls see at night.

How Do Polaroid Sunglasses Work?

WHAT YOU NEED:

- piece of window glass 30 cm square
- polaroid sunglasses
- fine wire 12 cm long
- daylight

WHAT HAPPENS IN THIS ACTIVITY?

You experiment with polarized light and make a model.

Light is made up of many waves which move through space. Even though the light travels in a straight line, each wave also vibrates in a sideways motion across the wave. These vibrations take place in all possible directions. Imagine a moving zig zag. We see light rays from a flashlight, for example, traveling forward. But the vibrations that make up these rays are at right angles to the forward-moving light. In certain conditions these vibrations can all be "captured" in one plane or one direction. The light is then said to be polarized.

Figure 1a.

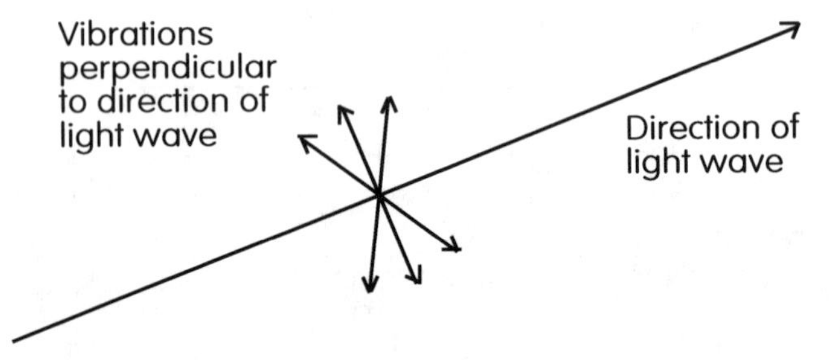

Figure 1b.

With polaroid sunglasses the horizontally vibrating light is blocked. If you put two lenses over one another at right angles, all light is blocked.

WHAT TO DO:

1. Hold the window glass in front of you in bright daylight at about the angle shown. As you do this, look at the glass through a polaroid sunglass lens, rotating the lens and experimenting with the angle at which you are holding the glass. You should be able to find a position where the light is cut off. This is because the light reflected by the glass is polarized, vibrating in one direction. When you rotate the polarizing lens, it cuts off the light from the glass.

Figure 2.

WHAT TO DO:

2. Next, look down at a piece of glossy white paper with typed print on it. Find the angle at which the glare reaches your eyes. Try to read the printing. You might have difficulty. Why is this? Now hold your polaroid filter between your eyes and the glaring surface. Figure 3.

~ You should be able to read the words now. Can you explain why?

Figure 3.

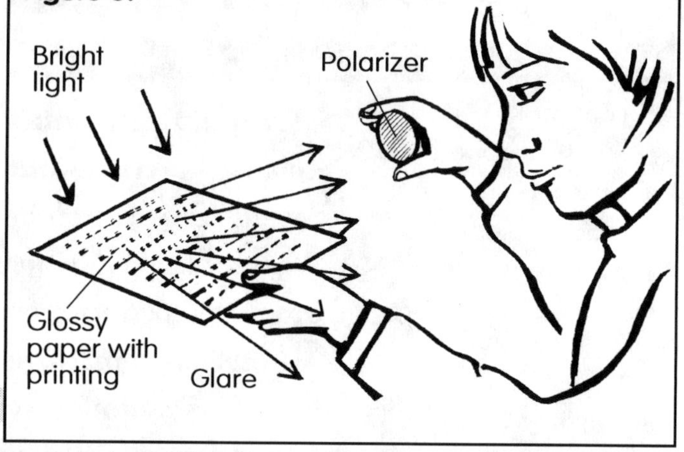

FURTHER INVESTIGATIONS:

Figure 4a.

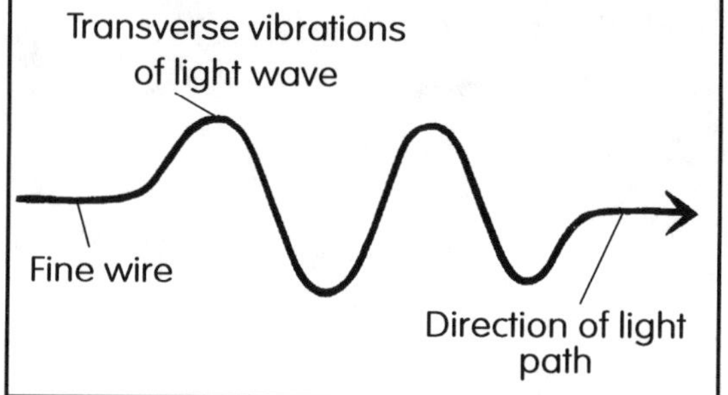

Figure 4b. Model Polarizer

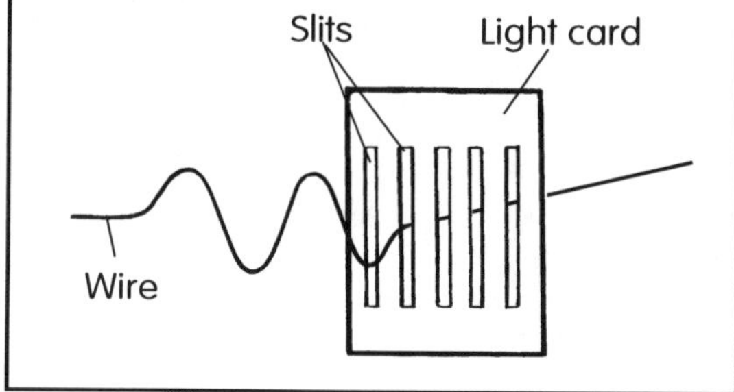

- You can make a model to show how polarization works. To do this, take a piece of fine wire and bend it to form a small model light wave as in Figure 4a. Make the waves about 1 cm deep. The curves representing the vibrations of the light ray are at right angles to its straight path, which is shown by the straight pieces of wire at the ends. In certain conditions, vibrations of the light may all be in one plane. The light is then said to be plane polarized.
- Now pass your wire light ray through your first model polarizing filter (Figure 4b.) and then through the second. The polarized light from the first model passes easily through the second, whose molecules are now parallel to those of the first model. Figure 5a.
- Now turn the second polarizer so that its slits are at right angles to those of the first model polarizer. Can you now pass your model light ray through both model polarizers?
- Relate this to your first two experiments and write out an explanation.

Figure 5a.

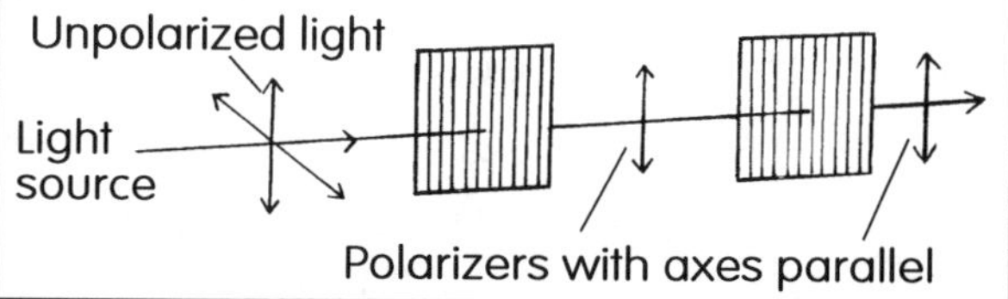

Figure 5b.

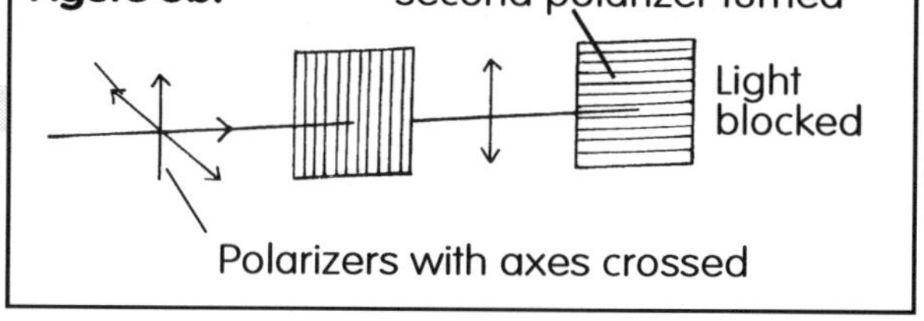

Let's Investigate
LIGHT
ACTIVITY 10:

Make a Magic Lantern!

WHAT YOU NEED:

- cardboard carton
- small cardboard box
- scissors
- reading glass
- two lamps
- colored magazine illustrations
- tape
- stapler

WHAT HAPPENS IN THIS ACTIVITY?

You make a magic lantern and demonstrate how it works.

With a magic lantern you can project colored pictures out of magazines onto a wall. This simple form of projection used to fascinate people over 100 years ago. It's fun to develop your own lantern, but it will also show you something important about focal length.

This is how it works:

When the illustration AB in Figure 1 is held at a distance from the lens greater than the focal length, another image forms beyond the focal length on the other side of the lens. The image is enlarged, upside down and in color.

Figure 1.

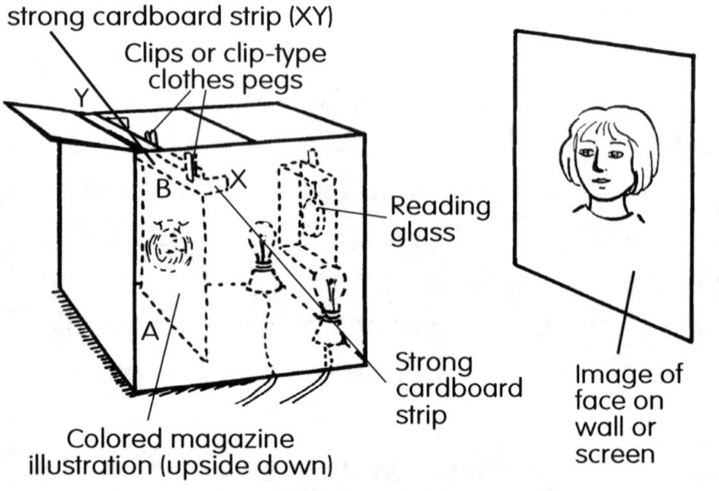

WHAT TO DO:

1. Select a cardboard carton in which one side is a little longer than the focal length of the reading glass (often about 20 cm). At one end of the box, in the center, cut out a circle of cardboard a little smaller than the diameter of the reading glass. Then in the small cardboard box, cut a hole just the right size to take the reading glass. Use tape to fasten the reading glass over both holes.

Figure 2.

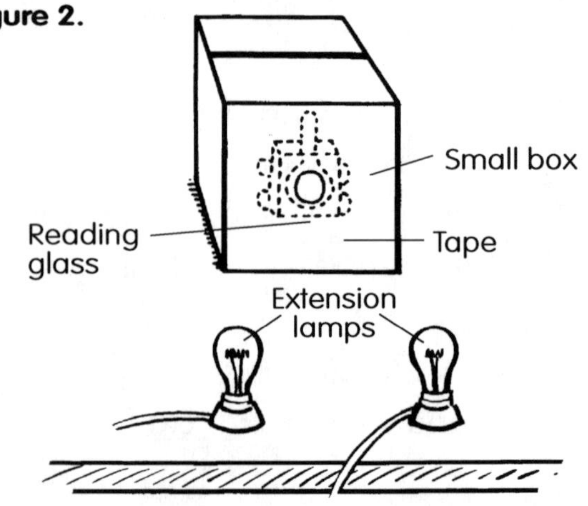

WHAT TO DO:

2. Place the two lamps on either side of the box as shown. Staple or tape in a strong strip of cardboard at XY as shown in Figure 1. Using clips or clip-type clothes pins, hang your illustrations upside down for projection. A dark room is necessary.

FURTHER INVESTIGATIONS:

- What have you learned about focal length from this activity?
- In Figure 3 draw in the light rays showing how the image of the tree is formed.
- Put on a slide show for your friends with your magic lantern.

Figure 3.

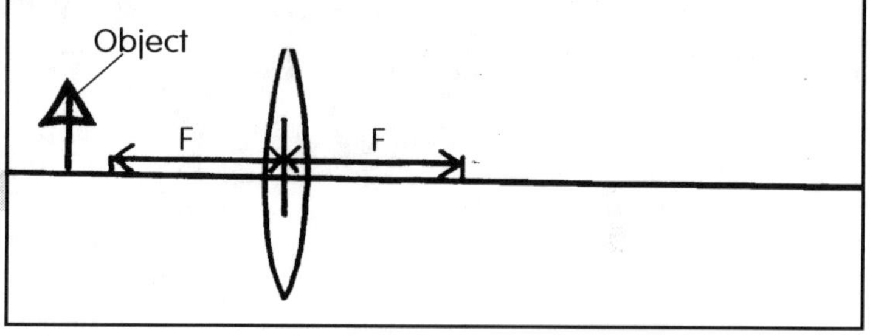

What Did the Astronauts Leave Behind?

WHAT YOU NEED:

- 2 flat mirrors 10 × 5 cm
- black paper
- white card
- plasticine or modelling clay
- tape
- paper cutter
- ruler
- pocket flashlight
- tipped lamp
- darkened room

WHAT HAPPENS IN THIS ACTIVITY?

You can show how a retroreflector works.

Some American and Russian spacecraft landing on the moon left retroreflectors there. Retroreflectors contain mirrors that reflect light back in exactly the direction from which it came. Scientists can fire powerful laser beams at the moon and then, using retroreflectors, detect the return laser pulses. By accurate timing of the round trip, it is possible to work out the earth-moon distance within an accuracy of centimeters!

Measurements with retroreflectors give us a better understanding of how the earth-moon gravity system works and of any irregularities in the earth's rotation, our basis of time.

Figure 1.

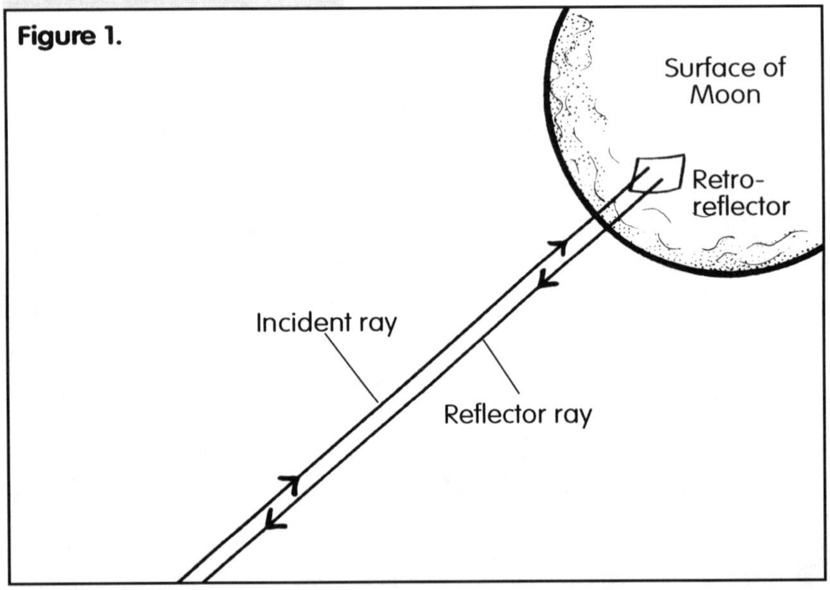

Figure 1. A retroreflector, as left by astronauts on the moon, is an instrument which causes reflected rays to return along paths parallel to those of their corresponding incident rays. One type used for light rays is the retrodirective mirror. Another kind, called a corner reflector, makes a useful radar target.

WHAT TO DO:

1. Cut a thin slit in a piece of black paper. Tape it to the front of a flashlight. Trim it as necessary.

Figure 2.

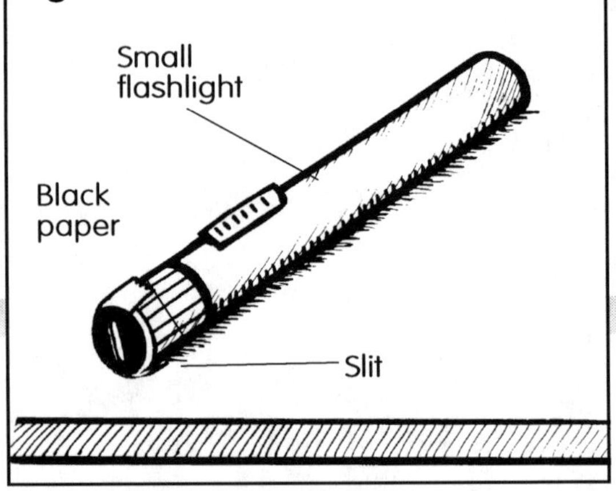

WHAT TO DO:

2. Tape the edges of the mirrors together to form a hinge so that you can open and close them. Fix the white card to the table-top with plasticine to form a screen.
3. Let the light from the torch strike one of the mirrors at an angle. Adjust the angle of the second mirror until you get a reflection on the screen.

Figure 3.

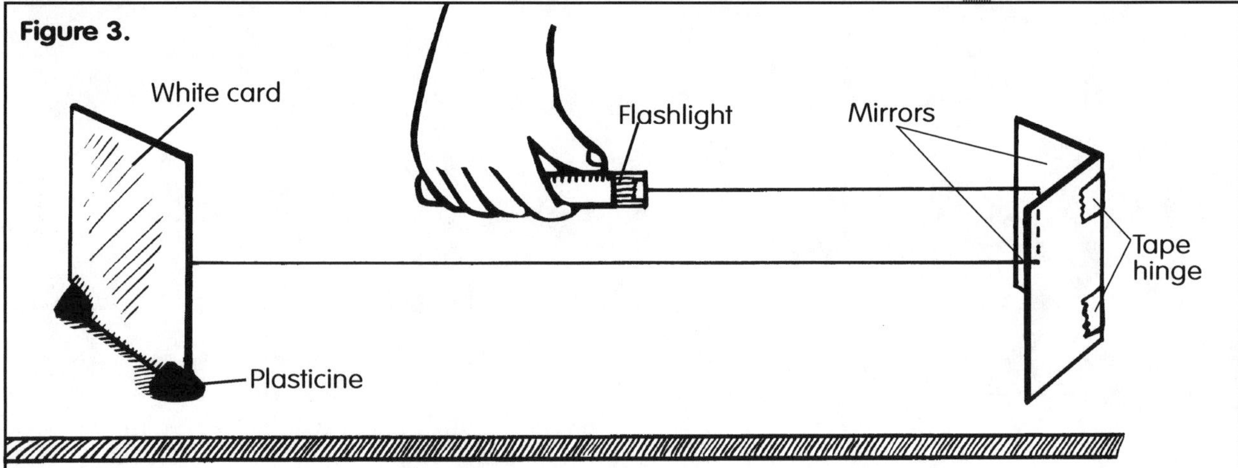

4. What do you observe? How does your experiment show the principle of the retroreflector as left by astronauts on the moon?

FURTHER INVESTIGATIONS:

- Research how the retroreflector was developed and how it works.
- Find out how retroreflectors left on the moon have been used by scientists.

COLOR

What Is Color?

Can You Transmit Colors?

Can You Change Colors?

Why Do We See Afterimages?

How Do You Mix Pigments?

Let's Investigate
COLOR
ACTIVITY 12:

What Is Color?

WHAT YOU NEED:

- cardboard disc with 5-6 mm hole at center
- plastic top of felt-tip pen
- string
- paper discs (white and colored) with slit and hole (see Figure 1)
- jelly crystals in various colors
- shallow dish
- spoon
- scissors
- template—supplied (Figure 3)
- colored paper
- wire holder
- removable tape

WHAT HAPPENS IN THIS ACTIVITY?

You experiment with the properties of color.

Color has three definite properties: hue, brightness and saturation. ***Hue*** *is the part of the spectrum of colors we call red, yellow, green, blue, purple and so on.* ***Brightness*** *is the amount of light the color seems to give off and explains why one color looks lighter or darker than another. This effect depends upon the observer and is different from person to person.* ***Saturation*** *is how pure a color is and depends upon the amount of white light a color contains. The more white light, the less saturated the color.*

There are two types of colors: primary and secondary. The primary colors are red, blue and yellow. All other colors (secondary colors) are made from varying mixtures of two primary colors. Black and white are not considered to be colors. Black absorbs all light, white reflects all light.

Figure 1.

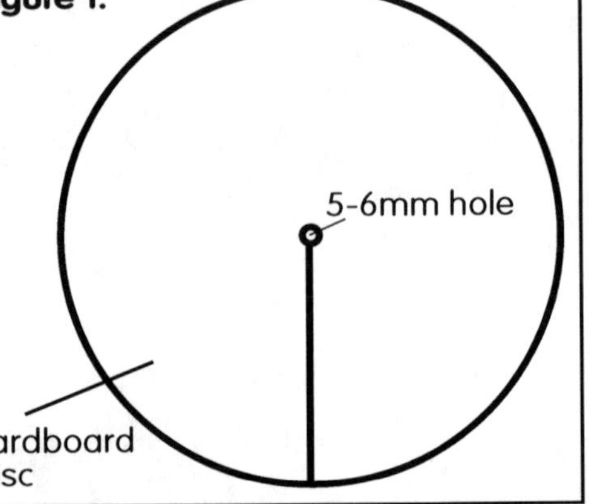

*Tiny pieces of removable tape placed at points along the outer edge of the disc will prevent any slipping of the discs as they spin.

WHAT TO DO:

1. Make a color top by placing a red paper disc over the cardboard disc and then slipping the plastic pen top through the center hole. This should fix the colored disc to the cardboard disc.*
2. Spin your top by running string around the plastic top, keeping this upright by the wire holder as in Figure 2. Pull evenly and firmly on the string and note the shade as the top spins. Now add the white disc by slipping the white edge under the red slot so that only a small section of the white shows. Spin the top.
   ~ What happens to the color? Gradually increase the amount of white. What happens to the color now, in terms of saturation?

Figure 2.

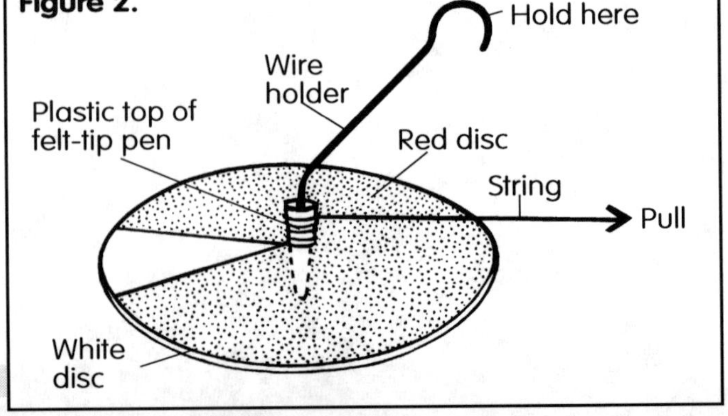

WHAT TO DO:

3. Try spinning the blue and yellow discs. Vary the amounts. What do you get? Try red, green and blue; then try red/blue, red/green, green/blue. Note the colors from each pair.
4. Now demonstrate color saturation with jelly crystals. Place some red jelly crystals in a shallow dish and crush them with the back of a spoon to make them finer and finer. What happens to the color as the particles become finer?
5. As the surface areas of the crystals increase, more and more white light is reflected. How does this affect saturation?
   ~ Try jelly crystals of other colors and make a report on your findings.
6. Cut strips 1 × 4 cm from your red and blue colored papers. Paste the red strip into space "x" in Figure 3 and the blue strip into space "y." Then face away from the incoming light and hold the page about 30 cm from your eyes. Write down what you see.
7. Colors of longer wavelengths seem to be closer than those of shorter wavelengths. Red is described as an **advancing** color and blue as **receding** color. When you are out in a car at night, look at whether the red or green traffic lights seem to be closer as you approach them.

Figure 3.

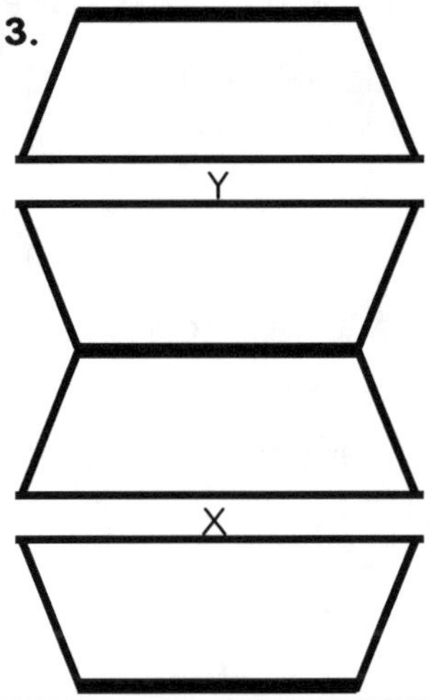

FURTHER INVESTIGATIONS:

- Stand in a light room with a dimmer switch. Look at a range of colors as you dim the light and note the sequence in which the colors disappear. How might this affect an astronaut or astronomer in the judgment of colors?
- Place the red and blue papers on a black sheet about 5cm apart. Take them into a room dark enough for the colors to disappear. Have your eyes fixed on the papers. As they adapt to the dark, note which color appears first. Shorter wavelength colors become visible more quickly as compared with those of longer wavelengths.

Let's Investigate
COLOR
ACTIVITY 13:

Can You Transmit Colors?

WHAT YOU NEED:

- 4 pieces cardboard 10 x 4 cm
- roundhead paper fastener
- color filters red, green, blue, yellow
- scissors
- tape
- colored papers
- black paper
- white paper

WHAT HAPPENS IN THIS ACTIVITY?

You experiment with filters and transmit colors.

Filters are devices used to modify light. You have probably seen their effect if you've ever been to a stage show. Filters are discs of colored glass, plastic or gelatine which transmit light of their own color and absorb light of other colors. For example, a photographer taking a picture of a landscape might use a yellow filter to prevent over-exposure of a blue sky and show greater detail in clouds. Astronomers use filters to cut down the moon's glare in lunar observations. Special color filters are used bring out hard-to-see details in planets.

WHAT TO DO:

1. Make a fan-like holder for the filters as in Figure 1. Tape each filter to the cardboard and fix the free ends together with a roundhead paper fastener.

Figure 1.

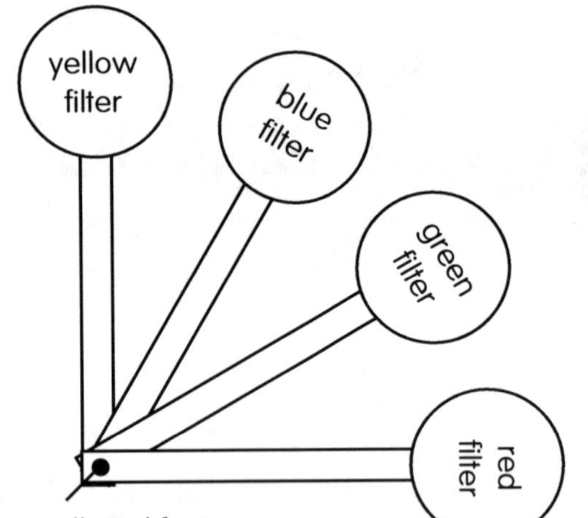

2. With the filters spread apart, allow a bright light to pass through them. What color does each filter transmit? What happens to the other colors?
3. Holding your filters about 25 cm before your eyes and with your back to the sun, look at the clear blue sky. Name the colors you see. **NEVER LOOK AT THE SUN THROUGH THE FILTERS!** It would damage your eyes!

WHAT TO DO:

4. Place the blue filter over the yellow and look at the sky again.
   ~ What color do you now see? Now place the green over the other two and then the red. Explain how the colors are successively subtracted.
5. Place colored papers on a black background under bright light. Look at them through your filters. Which colors appear black or dark grey? After studying Figure 2, explain why.

Figure 2.

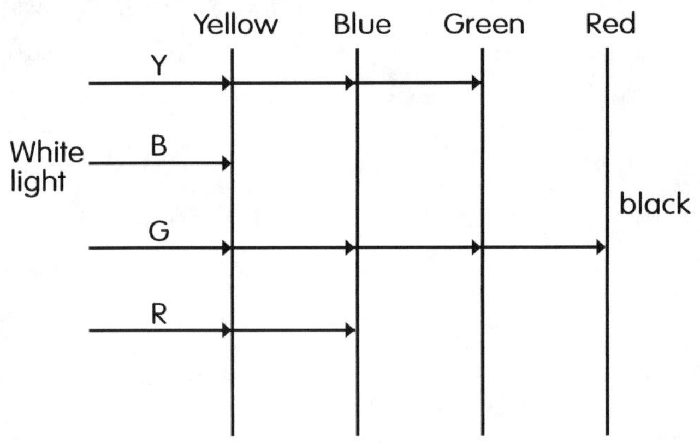

FURTHER INVESTIGATIONS:

- In bright daylight, look through your red filter at white paper and then at the sky. Which red looks brighter? Can you say why?
- Now turn your back on the light and look at your red filter. Can you explain why it looks darker, almost black? Repeat with other filters.
- Go outside and look at the great variety of nature's colors through your filters. What would the world look like if there were no green?
- Research what color-blindness is.

Let's Investigate
COLOR
ACTIVITY 14:

Can You Change Colors?

WHAT YOU NEED:

- prism
- large sheet of cardboard
- mirror
- basin of water
- chalk dust or white powder (e.g., plaster of Paris)
- color illustrations
- colored cellophane
- card 20 × 15 cm
- paper of different colors
- paper cutter or scissors
- dark room

WHAT HAPPENS IN THIS ACTIVITY?

You experiment with changing colors.

Take a prism or three-sided piece of glass from a hanging lamp and hold it so that sunlight falls on one of the sides. A beautiful rainbow, or spectrum of colors, should form on the wall or ceiling. This is because sunlight contains different wavelengths. Because each wave travels at a different speed, when the sun's rays pass through the glass, each ray is bent to a different degree. As a result the waves spread, or fan out. They may leave the prism to enter the eye directly or reflect to the eye from a white wall showing as a band of rainbow colors.

Round water drops can also break light up into many kinds of waves and produce a rainbow. Water drops in clouds act as prisms, refracting or bending the rays of sunlight, then reflecting them from the back of the drop and refracting the rays again as they leave the drop. The angle between the ray from the sun entering the drop and the ray coming to our eye is about 42°. In this activity, you form a water wedge made by a mirror and water surface. This acts as a three-sided prism breaking sunlight up into a spectrum just as a glass prism does.

Figure 1.

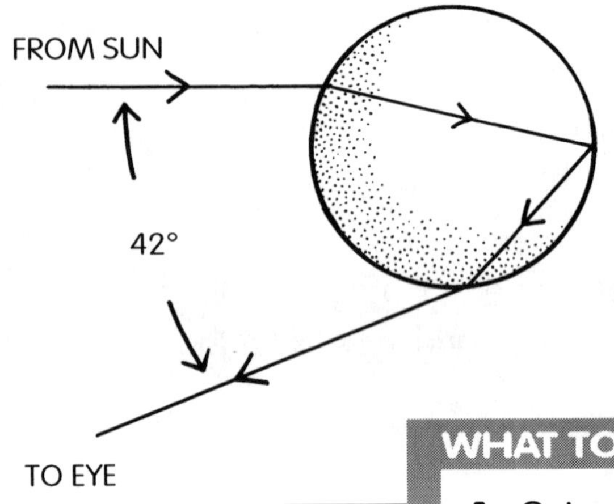

WHAT TO DO:

1. Cut a slit about 10 × 5 cm in the large piece of cardboard for the sun's rays to pass through. Then tape the cardboard to the window. Use curtains as necessary to keep the room dark. Allow a beam of sunlight to fall on the mirror in the basin full of water. Figure 2.
   - ~ What do you observe on the wall? Describe the colors in order.
   - ~ What is the scientific name for the rainbow band of colors?

Figure 2.

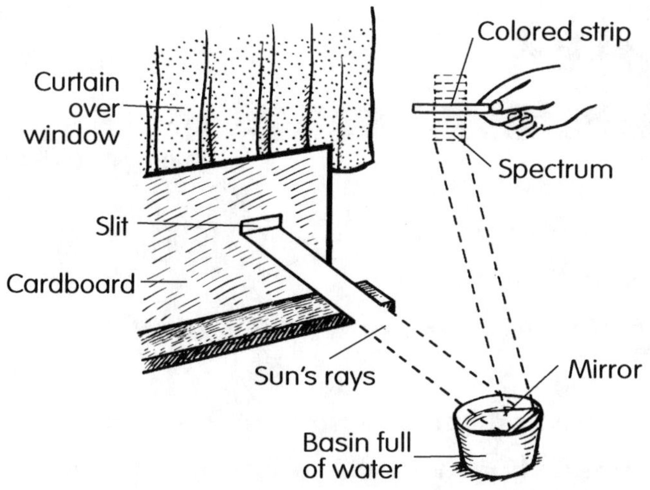

WHAT TO DO:

2. Shake or sprinkle some white dust in front of the spectrum.
   ~ What do you notice about the dust particles?
3. Cut strips 15 x 1.5 cm of a different colors. Hold each strip in turn in each color of the spectrum. What do you notice about each strip?
4. Hold 2-3 sheets of cellophane of one color over the slit.
   ~ What do you notice about the spectrum?
5. Repeat with cellophane sheets of another color and record your results.
   ~ Write a paragraph entitled "Changing Colors."

FURTHER INVESTIGATIONS:

- Look at some "iridescent" colors in a mother of pearl object, turning them at different angles. Describe the colors. See if you can find out how the colors are made. Find out where the word "iridescent" comes from and what it means.
- How are metallic colors made?
- Collect a variety of color sample cards from paint shops. Classify them into warm, cold, fresh, loud and soft colors. How do you think colors came to be associated with feelings?
- What spotlights would you use at a school drama to make the yellow clothes of the actors appear black?

Let's Investigate **COLOR**

ACTIVITY 15:

Why Do We See Afterimages?

WHAT YOU NEED:

- colored squares of paper about 8 cm^2 in various colors
- sheet of white paper

WHAT HAPPENS IN THIS ACTIVITY?

You experiment with changing colors.

While we are not normally aware of it, the image of an object in our eyes does not disappear at the instant the object is removed but persists for a short time. This image is known as an afterimage.

Motion pictures are based on this phenomenon as shown in Figure 1. It is considered that this type of afterimage (or persistence of vision) exists because the brain continues to receive messages from the retina after the object has been taken away. Moving pictures do not actually move but in each frame of the film, the action is advanced slightly. By projecting the film sufficiently rapidly, the observer sees continuous movement.

When you look at the green square in the following activity, the receptors for green in the retina tire and so decrease in sensitivity. But the receptors for red and blue are not stimulated. So when you look at the white background, which reflects all colors, the tired green receptors do not respond, but the red and blue receptors do. This results in a magenta afterimage. The colors we observe as afterimages are colors complementary to the original colors.*

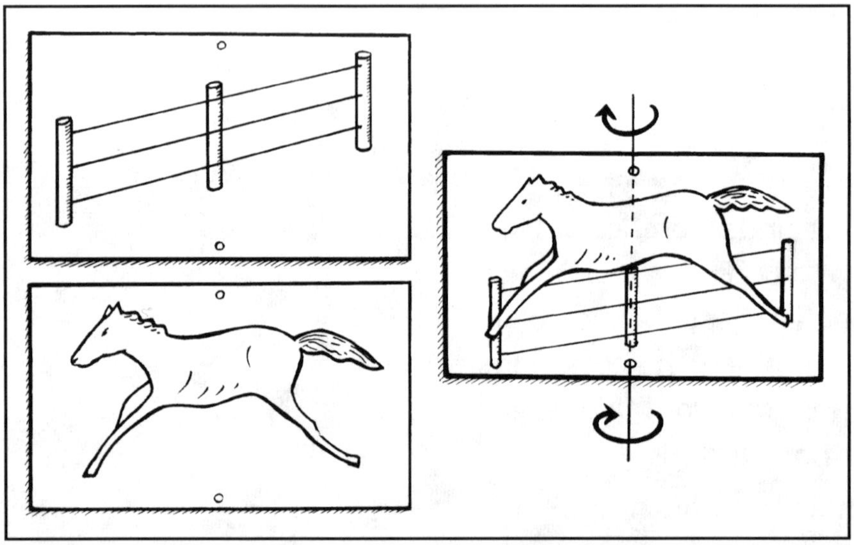

Figure 1. If you cut out the two drawings, paste them back to back on a piece of card and twirl them, you will see the horse jumping the fence. This is an afterimage effect. Try experimenting with it in color.

*red-blue or shade of purple

WHAT TO DO:

1. Look at a bright light for a few seconds, then close your eyes.
   ~ What do you see? This type of afterimage which appears the same in color and in shape as the object is called a positive afterimage.
2. Place a square of green paper in the middle of the white sheet of paper and look closely for a full minute (count slowly to 60). Now quickly look at a blank white background. What color do you see?
   ~ How is this color related to the original green. Can you explain why?
3. Look at a square of red paper for a similar time then look at the blank white background. What color do you see? How are the colors related?
4. Repeat for a blue square, a yellow square, and other colors. Keep a record of your afterimages.

FURTHER INVESTIGATIONS:

- What makes the sky blue?
- Why does the sky become bluer at high altitudes?
- Seen from the moon, what is the color of the sky? Explain why.

Why Do You Mix Pigments?

WHAT YOU NEED:

- Box of pigments or paints
- brushes
- water
- white card
- colored squares of paper: red, blue, green, yellow, black and white

WHAT HAPPENS IN THIS ACTIVITY?

You experiment at mixing pigments.

You already know that you can't see colors without light and that seeing different colors simply means that you are seeing light traveling at different wavelengths. If you mix two light colors together, the resulting color is always brighter than either of the original colors.

When you obtain colors by mixing paints or pigments, the resulting color is always the result of subtraction. This is because in subtractive mixing, light is absorbed and the final color is darker. In Figure 1, red, green, and blue are known as the additive primaries. The colors showing in between—yellow, cyan, and magenta—are called the subtractive primaries. When you combine the additive primaries, they produce white; when you combine the subtractive primaries, they produce black.

Figure 1. Additive color mixing, as for example, projecting the three additive primary colors onto a screen.

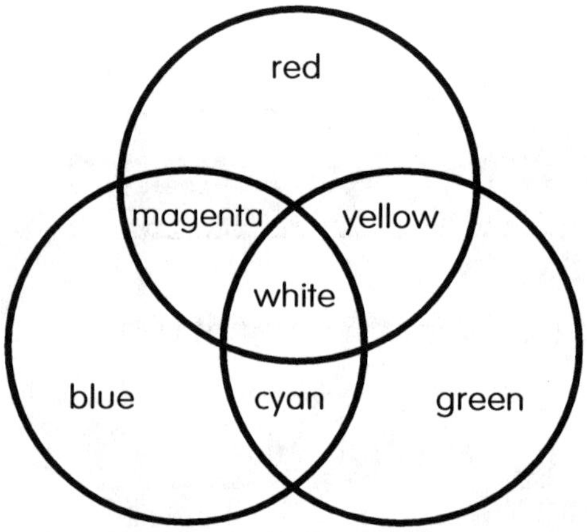

Figure 2. The color wheel and complementary colors.

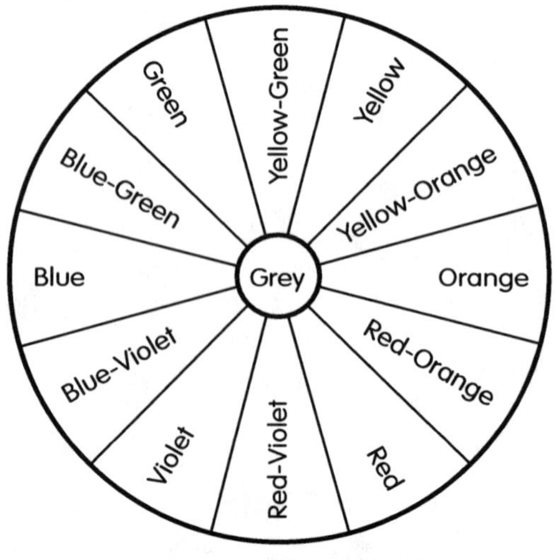

COLOR THEORY: THE COLOR WHEEL AND COMPLEMENTARY COLORS

When two colors mixed in the right amounts give grey, they are called complementary colors. Red and green, as shown on the color wheel in Figure 2, are complementary colors; so are red-violet and yellow-green. Using the color wheel you can get exactly the same grey in many different ways. The primary colors are the 3 pigment colors that cannot be formed by the combination of any others: red, yellow and blue. All other colors are formed by combining these colors.

WHAT TO DO:

1. On a piece of white card, try mixing blue and yellow paints.
   ~ What color do you get? Can you explain why?

   If a yellow paint absorbs all the colors of the spectrum except red, green and yellow and a blue absorbs all spectral colors except blue and green, then on mixing the two together the only color to be reflected by both is green. The resulting color is what is left over after subtraction. Figure 4.

2. Try mixing the three subtractive primary colors together using pigments or paints. What do you get? Explain why.

Figure 4. If blue and yellow paints are mixed together, then green is the only color reflected by the two pigments. Some yellow may be transmitted.

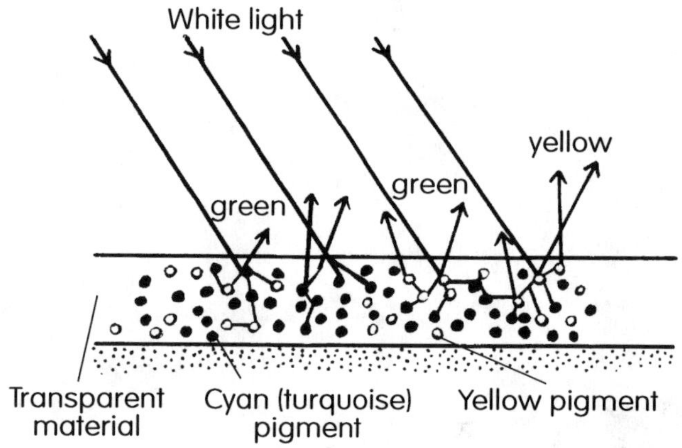

FURTHER INVESTIGATIONS:

- Try adding white in varying amounts to the three subtractive colors in combination. You will find you can get practically any color you desire.
- Look at your red paper. Why is it red?
- Look at this white paper? What light wavelengths are reflected? Look at the black paper and/or this print. What light is absorbed? If black absorbs all wavelengths, then how is it you can see the type?